Hell Itself

THE BATTLE OF THE WILDERNESS, MAY 5-7, 1864

by Chris Mackowski

EMERGING CIVIL WAR SERIES

Chris Mackowski, series editor
Christopher Kolakowski, chief historian

The Emerging Civil War Series

offers compelling, easy-to-read overviews of some of the Civil War's most important battles and issues.

Recipient of the Army Historical Foundation's Lieutenant General Richard G. Trefry Award for contributions to the literature on the history of the U.S. Army

Other titles in the Emerging Civil War Series include:

Bloody Autumn: The Shenandoah Valley Campaign of 1864
   by Daniel T. Davis and Phillip S. Greenwalt

Calamity in Carolina: The Battles of Averasboro and Bentonville, March 1865
   by Daniel T. Davis and Phillip S. Greenwalt

Don't Give an Inch: The Second Day at Gettysburg—From Little Round Top to Cemetery Ridge, July 2, 1863
   by Chris Mackowski, Kristopher D. White, and Daniel T. Davis

Fight Like the Devil: The First Day at Gettysburg, July 1, 1863
   by Chris Mackowski, Kristopher D. White, and Daniel T. Davis

Grant's Last Battle: The Story Behind the Personal Memoirs of Ulysses S. Grant
   by Chris Mackowski

Hurricane from the Heavens: The Battle of Cold Harbor, May 26-June 5, 1864
   by Daniel T. Davis and Phillip S. Greenwalt

The Last Days of Stonewall Jackson: The Mortal Wounding of the Confederacy's Greatest Icon
   by Chris Mackowski and Kristopher D. White

Out Flew the Sabres: The Battle of Brandy Station, June 9, 1863
   by Eric J. Wittenberg and Daniel T. Davis

A Season of Slaughter: The Battle of Spotsylvania Court House, May 8-21, 1864
   by Chris Mackowski and Kristopher D. White

Simply Murder: The Battle of Fredericksburg, December 13, 1862
   by Chris Mackowski and Kristopher D. White

That Furious Struggle: Chancellorsville and the High Tide of the Confederacy, May 1-5, 1863
   by Chris Mackowski and Kristopher D. White

For a complete list of titles in the Emerging Civil War Series, visit www.emergingcivilwar.com

Hell Itself

THE BATTLE OF THE WILDERNESS, MAY 5-7, 1864

by Chris Mackowski

EMERGING CIVIL WAR SERIES

SB

Savas Beatie
California

For Lee Coppola and Dr. Pauline "P-Ho" Hoffmann

Second edition, first printing

ISBN-13 (paperback): 978-1-61121-315-7
ISBN-13 (ebook): 978-1-61121-316-4

Library of Congress Cataloging-in-Publication Data

Names: Mackowski, Chris, author.
Title: Hell itself : the Battle of the Wilderness, May 5-7, 1864 / by Chris Mackowski.
Description: First edition. | El Dorado Hills, California : Savas Beatie, 2016. | Series: Emerging Civil War series | Includes bibliographical references and index.
Identifiers: LCCN 2016010812| ISBN 9781611213157 (pbk : alk. paper) | ISBN 9781611213164 (ebk. : alk. paper)
Subjects: LCSH: Wilderness, Battle of the, Va., 1864.
Classification: LCC E476.52 .M339 2016 | DDC 973.7/36--dc23
LC record available at http://lccn.loc.gov/2016010812

Published by

SB Savas Beatie LLC
989 Governor Drive, Suite 102
El Dorado Hills, California 95762
Phone: 916-941-6896
Email: sales@savasbeatie.com
Web: www.savasbeatie.com

MIX
Paper from responsible sources
FSC® C011935

Savas Beatie titles are available at special discounts for bulk purchases in the United States by corporations, institutions, and other organizations. For more details, please contact Special Sales, 989 Governor Drive, Suite 102, El Dorado Hills, CA 95762, or you may e-mail us as at sales@savasbeatie.com, or visit our website at www.savasbeatie.com for additional information.

This limited special edition is published in cooperation with the American Battlefield Trust.

AMERICAN BATTLEFIELD TRUST ★ ★ ★

PRESERVE. EDUCATE. INSPIRE.

Special Preservation Edition Foreword

We had a run for it. Staff officers yelling and calling on the men to rally and support the artillery and the men throwing their guns and running like mad men and them Rebs a yelling as they came up on the charge with that peculiar yell they have. It sounded like a lot of school boys let loose. I thought Hell had broke loose.

Samuel Bradbury, Union Army Engineer
in a letter home following the Battle of the Wilderness

As a dedicated preservationist and student of our nation's history, you know that every battlefield has stories to tell. The Wilderness is no exception. It was on this field —in the dense forests and impenetrable thickets of rural Virginia—that General U.S. Grant and General Robert E. Lee faced each other for the first time.

If you have visited the Wilderness or any other battlefield, for that matter, I'm sure you understand the critical importance of experiencing our nation's hallowed ground firsthand—walking the ground gives a glimpse of what soldiers had to contend with and brings a battle to life in ways nothing else can. To traverse the land, to walk in the very footsteps of those who fought and fell, is a poignant experience.

To date, preservationists like you have added more than 259 acres to the Wilderness Battlefield, ensuring that present and future generations will be able to learn from and explore this unparalleled outdoor classroom. The Wilderness represents one of the many battlefields in America that constantly faces the threat of development, but recently, you have helped to ensure that an additional 36-acre tract will never suffer that fate.

Hell Itself: The Battle of the Wilderness, May 5-7, 1864 helps us understand the enduring importance of this battle, and reminds us that we can always enrich and deepen our understanding of the events that shaped our nation. Long after the bullets have ceased to whistle through the trees, and long after the fires that swept with such terrifying fury through the underbrush there were extinguished–the preserved land, as well as the stories of the people who hallowed that ground, continue to teach us about who we are and why we are the way we are.

The American Battlefield Trust is proud to partner with Savas Beatie to produce 1,864 "special preservation" copies of this work, available to our members all across America, each of whom has contributed to the preservation of this important battlefield. Please be sure to visit our website at battlefields.org/visit/battlefields/wilderness-battlefield to learn even more about the battle, to download a free Battle App so that you can tour the battlefield on your smartphone, watch an animated map or two, and learn how you can help save even more of our history.

Thank you once more for supporting the mission of the American Battlefield Trust. Your generosity preserves priceless hallowed ground, educates millions about our nation's history, and inspires people to become better citizens, which will make us a stronger and more unified nation.

With warmest regards,

David Duncan
President

Table of Contents

Footnotes for this volume are available at
http://emergingcivilwar.com/publications/the-emerging-civil-war-series/footnotes

* * *

List of Maps

Maps by Hal Jespersen

Acknowledgments

Proceeds from the sale of this book support battlefield preservation.

My foremost thanks go to John Hennessy, who first asked me to write about the Wilderness in 2010 and who allowed me to return to the Wilderness for this volume. Both experiences were immensely gratifying. I also thank Greg Mertz, the man who first opened my eyes to this oft-overlooked and underappreciated battle. I'm honored to have him contribute the foreword to this volume.

Ellwood is filled to the rafters with history and stories. (cm)

I am also grateful for the contributions Dan Davis, Gregg Kneipp, Rebekah Oakes, and Ryan Quint made to the appendices of this book.

Eric Mink, Noel Harrison, and Don Pfanz provided materials and research assistance that were absolutely critical to this book. Don also offered invaluable editorial assistance in the manuscript's earliest form. I am deeply indebted to each of them and am fortunate to have them as friends.

I also thank Josef Rokus for his contributions on the civilians of the Wilderness, and Carolyn Elstner for her background information on Ellwood. Thanks, too, to Janice Frye, Joe Obidzinski, Fran Smith, and Frank O'Reilly.

With Savas Beatie, thanks to Theodore Savas, Sarah

Keeney, Yvette Lewis, and the rest of the excellent staff, who all always do such a nice job for the ECWS. For this volume, in particular, Kailyn Jennings offered helpful copyediting.

Gordon Rhea's book *The Battle of the Wilderness: May 5-6, 1864* is not only the most exhaustive study of the battle, it's also highly readable. Gordon's work remains profoundly inspiring to me as a writer. He writes history the way it's meant to be written.

At St. Bonaventure University's Russell J. Jandoli of Journalism and Mass Communication, I thank the dean, Pauline Hoffmann. Professors Patrick Vecchio and Carole McNall; our former colleague, John Hanchette; and our former dean, Lee Coppola, all lent support in various ways to the earlier version of this book. Thanks, too, to John Cummings, Jackson Foster, and the Friends of Fredericksburg Area Battlefields for their support of that earlier version. Thanks, too, to Heidi Hartley.

Most importantly, I thank my kids, Stephanie and Jackson, and my wife, Jennifer. The Wilderness never feels so wild knowing I have them to come home to.

Kris White made many valuable contributions to this volume. My best times in the Wilderness have been spent with Kris, who's tromped away many an hour with me on the battlefield. Together, we've smoked a lot of cigars; unraveled the mysteries around James Longstreet's wounding; watched the *Hindenburg* crash onto the *Titanic* (metaphorically, anyway); heard the legendary growl of Ed Bearrs sending Lee to the rear; and more. Wild times, indeed.

*   *   *

Portions of *Hell Itself: The Battle of the Wilderness* previously appeared in *The Dark, Close Wood: Ellwood, the Wilderness, and the Battle that Transformed Both* by Chris Mackowski. (Thomas Publications, 2010). The text in the current volume, which has been significantly expanded, also includes new interpretive sections, appendices, more than 150 photos, and eleven original maps.

A longer version of Appendix D, co-authored with Kristopher D. White, appeared as "Unfriendly Fire" in the May 2009 issue of *America's Civil War*.

PHOTO CREDITS:
Fredericksburg and Spotsylvania National Military Park (fsnmp); Jack Humphries (jh); Huntington Library, Art Collections, and Botanical Gardens (hl); Library of Congress (loc); Chris Mackowski (cm); *Photographic History of the Civil War* (phcw)

For the Emerging Civil War Series

Theodore P. Savas, *publisher*
Chris Mackowski, *series editor*
Christopher Kolakowski, *chief historian*
Sarah Keeney, *editorial consultant*
Kristopher D. White, *co-founding editor*

Maps by Hal Jespersen
Design and layout by Chris Mackowski

Touring the Battlefield

Because the battle of the Wilderness unfolded on two fronts, it is difficult to follow the battle chronologically while also following it geographically. The narrative of the book flows chronologically, and the tour route will ask visitors to do just a little extra driving in order

to better follow the action. Therefore, the tour route in this book sometimes mirrors the NPS route, but in other places it does not. Along the way, too, there are a few optional stops that can round out a visitor's experience. The text points out those places along the way. Also, while most chapters have a tour stop associated with them, a couple do not. The text will provide directions as necessary.

The tour suggests Ellwood as a start point; however, because Ellwood is open seasonally, it might be necessary to start at the Chancellorsville Battlefield Visitor Center along Route 3. There, visitors can get an off-season pass to walk the grounds of Ellwood, even when the building itself is closed. Otherwise, the Route 3/Route 20 intersection provides a convenient point of reference for starting the tour. Both roads, as well as the Brock Road and Plank Road, can be extremely busy, so please exercise caution.

An NPS historian shares Ellwood's stories with visitors. Volunteers from a robust friends group, Friends of Wilderness Battlefield, also provide tours and programming. (cm)

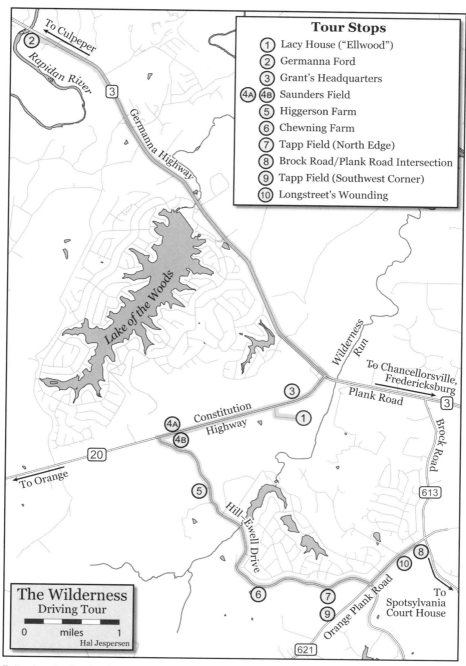

Following the battle of the Wilderness, the armies moved on to Spotsylvania Court House, just 10 miles down Brock Road. Pick up that phase of the story in *A Season of Slaughter: The Battle of Spotsylvania Court House, May 8-21, 1864* by Chris Mackowski and Kristopher D. White, part of the Emerging Civil War Series.

Foreword

BY GREGORY A. MERTZ

Mentioning the battle of the Wilderness to even the most casual student of the Civil War instantly conjures two particular distinctions that separate it from other battles.

One unique aspect was that fires broke out and burned some of the casualties. A rain-deprived spring season and a densely wooded terrain covered by dry leaf litter turned the Wilderness into a tinderbox. The thick vegetation with limited visibility through the underbrush meant that the troops often fired at one another at close range. Exchanging rounds at short distances not only caused horrific casualties in the Wilderness, but the black-powder weapons spewed sparks and burning embers into an even-more compact area between the close opposing battle lines. Wildfires swept across the fields and through the woods. Dead men were burnt and horribly mangled when cartridge boxes exploded. Wounded men pushed leaf litter away from them so the inferno might somehow go around them. Veteran soldiers who thought they had seen the worst of the horrors war could offer now felt that witnessing the Wilderness wildfires engulf fallen soldiers was by far their most ghastly experience of the war. Many battlefields have examples of fires flaring up, but none were as dreadful as those of the Wilderness.

In addition to the raging flames, the second feature for which the battle of the Wilderness is most remembered is being the first battle to compete the two generals who were indisputably the two most talented soldiers produced by their respective armies: Ulysses S. Grant for the Federals and Robert E. Lee for the Confederates. It was the start of an 11-month chess match of masterful maneuver, attack, and counterattack that only concluded when the war itself had finally ended.

The Army of the Potomac rolled out of a long winter dormancy and into one of the worst nightmares the men had yet experienced in the war. (cm)

A consequence of the two talented and successful commanders going head to head in the Wilderness was that neither general would be completely fooled by the other, nor would either back down when the going got tough. At the conclusion of the battle, neither had achieved a clear-cut victory, though it would hardly be accurate to simply declare the battle of the Wilderness as a draw.

While fires broke out during several of the war's battles, none have become so notorious as those that blazed through the Wilderness. (loc)

The Confederates had achieved a tactical victory because they had inflicted a greater number of casualties upon the Federal forces than they had suffered themselves. Confederate losses are estimated to be just over 11,000 men, whereas the Federal troops officially suffered 17,666 killed, wounded, and missing. Lee's strategy throughout the war was to drive the Federal casualty numbers to such a point that the death and maiming would demoralize the northern populace and their elected officials. Lee wanted the despair to reach such a degree that the North would decide that the cost of forcing the Southern states to rejoin the Union was not worth it. During the battle of Spotsylvania Court House, which began only one day after the fight in the Wilderness, a Southern newspaper wrote of the lopsided number of casualties after the first week of combat between Lee and Grant, calling the Federal general a "butcher." Soon thereafter, northern newspapers were likewise complaining about the disparaging losses in Grant's army, utilizing the same analogy in also declaring Grant a "butcher." At the Wilderness and the subsequent battles, the Confederates could see they had obtained some advantages over their northern opponents in terms of casualty comparisons.

Amassing casualties in significantly greater numbers than his opponent was not a characteristic of Grant's battles prior to facing Lee and his Army of Northern Virginia in the Wilderness. In fact, Grant had gained his reputation for taking away the enemy's ability to wage war rather than exacting high tolls in killed and wounded upon the Confederates. The initials in "U.S. Grant" coincided with the terms he offered to the Fort Donelson, Tennessee, garrison, as he became known as "Unconditional Surrender" Grant. Grant had not battered the Confederate army into submission, but with help from the U.S. Navy, had surrounded the fort and forced its capitulation. Rather than inflict a large number of killed and wounded upon the Fort Donelson defenders, Grant captured some 12,000 men in February 1862. Then, utilizing maneuver and several small-scale battles, and once again with valuable assistance from the navy, Grant was able to force the Confederate army protecting Vicksburg, Mississippi, to surrender 30,000 soldiers on July 4, 1863.

Late in 1863, then-General-in-Chief Henry W. Halleck queried his talented field commander Grant as to what he would propose be done with the Army of the Potomac confronting Lee in Virginia. Not surprisingly, Grant suggested another campaign of attrition in which his objectives would be to take away Lee's ability to wage warfare. Grant proposed sending 30,000 men from the army to the coast of North Carolina then into the interior of the state with the state capitol of Raleigh as the objective. The Federal invasion force would serve the dual purpose of cutting key railroads that were sending supplies to Lee's army, while also prohibiting goods and weapons making it through the blockade into Wilmington and reaching the interior railroads for distribution.

In addition to hampering the Confederate supply system, Grant also felt the presence of a Federal army in the heart of North Carolina would discourage a part of the South's population that had not yet directly experienced the hard hand of war, and might spawn desertion among North Carolina soldiers in Lee's army who would want to defend their home state. Morale was already low among some of the Tar Heels serving under Lee, and many in the state were in a tizzy over the perceived lack of appreciation of North Carolina troops. Such sentiment grew from the aftermath of the October 14, 1863, battle of Bristoe Station, Virginia, in which Virginia General A.P. Hill was soundly criticized for carelessly sending a pair of North Carolina brigades into a fray in which they were badly cut up.

Both of those actions—cutting supplies and denigrating the morale of the enemy—were methods of hampering the ability of the Confederates to conduct the war, rather than inflict significant casualties upon Confederate soldiers.

But Washington didn't like Grant's ideas. Halleck responded critically that reducing the number of troops in Lee's front would only enable him to go north again, duplicating what he had done in the Antietam and the Gettysburg Campaigns. When Lincoln conferred with Grant prior to naming him the General-in-Chief of all Federal armies to replace Halleck, he first asked if Grant could accept his requirement that the Army of the Potomac must be devoted to destroying Lee's army and making sure that, whenever it eventually withdrew to Richmond and the war developed into a siege, Lee would not have the strength to detach a force large enough to cause any havoc.

Though Grant's strategy had been quite successful and was a particularly good strategy for an army with superior resources and the ability to carry out a protracted war, 1864 was an election year, and if Lincoln had any hopes of returning to the White House for a second term, the voting populace had to perceive that Lincoln was winning the war. Eight months passed from the time Grant was appointed General-in-Chief to the fall presidential election. Lincoln did not have the time to wait for Grant's preferred strategy to work. Grant grasped the need to adopt a strategy that focused on the annihilation of Lee's army.

Though Grant was in charge of all Federal armies and might well have established his headquarters in Washington, the electorate whose fathers, sons, husbands, and brothers made up the Army of the Potomac demanded that the best Federal general be brought in to lead that hard-luck force. Grant, therefore, established his headquarters side by side with the army opposed to Robert E. Lee.

Plans for the spring campaign of 1864 revolved around passing to the east of Lee's army, a move around the Confederate right flank. The maneuver would take the army through a region known as the Wilderness. The thick woods and limited visibility would not enable the Federals to take advantage of their larger numbers of troops and superior artillery. The Federals did not intend to fight in the Wilderness, but rather pass *through* the Wilderness. Lee, however, had other ideas.

Hell Itself approaches the battle of the Wilderness in a format designed to tell that story where it can best be understood—while standing on the battlefield and seeing just where the events occurred as described in the book. This guidebook by Chris Mackowski blends his talent as an experienced public historian well accustomed to making the battlefield relevant to visitors with that of a journalism professional who knows just how to meld the right words together. Casual and serious students of the war alike will gain an understanding of the battle, its participants, and the unique landscape upon which the battle of the Wilderness was fought and its significance.

The 150th anniversary of the battle of the Wilderness in 2014 coincided by just a few days with my own 30th anniversary of working at the National Park that preserves and interprets the battlefield. It was remarkable to ponder the many changes for the better that have occurred over those 30 years. The ground of Longstreet's Flank Attack was threatened with

When the armies moved on the night of May 7, they left behind thousands of dead. Exact numbers of the dead were impossible to determine, but total Federal casualties totaled around 18,000; Confederates between 11,000-13,000. (loc)

development but has now been preserved. The most dramatic scene of the battle is arguably the "Lee to the Rear" episode in the Widow Tapp Field. The tiny cleared area around monuments commemorating that event was expanded into a full-fledged scenic restoration of the Tapp Field. New trails across the Tapp Field, throughout the maze of earthworks in the Gordon Flank Attack area, and around the Brock Road/Plank Road intersection give visitors an intimate look at key portions of the battlefield. The number of driving tour stops has expanded from three to eight points of interest. The shell of the historic structure Ellwood has been restored, supplemented with exhibits and seasonally staffed by volunteers—all due to the efforts of the Friends of Wilderness Battlefield.

Thirty years ago the most substantial book on the battle was a difficult read for even the student with the most intense passion to learn. Authors have now contributed to both the scholarship of the battle and provided us with well-written studies. *Hell Itself*, through its format, length, and writing style, provides yet another contribution to the literature by enabling everyone to share in the understanding of the battle of the Wilderness story.

All circumstances seemed to combine
to make the scene one of unutterable horror.
At times the wind howled through
the tree-tops, mingling its moans with
the groans of the dying, and heavy branches
were cut off by the fire of the artillery, and fell
crashing upon the heads of the men,
adding a new terror to battle. Forest fires
raged; ammunition trains exploded;
the dead were roasted in the conflagration;
the wounded, roused by its hot breath,
dragged themselves along with their torn
and mangled limbs, in the mad energy of
despair, to escape the ravages of the flames;
and every bush seemed hung with shreds of
blood-stained clothing. It seems as though
Christian men had turned to fiends, and
hell itself had usurped the place of earth.

— *Horace Porter*

The Present as Prologue

NOW

It's quiet there now in the simple frame house. No cannons boom. No muskets roar. No wounded cry for help.

No children laugh in the dooryard as they run and play. No cattle low. No horses whinny. No song drifts up from around the fire pit in front of the slave cabins.

Instead, a blue-tailed skink suns itself on the stone steps that lead up to the front porch, which looks out over the Wilderness Run valley. Once, a driveway looped up to the foot of the steps from the Parker's Store Road, but both the driveway and the road have disappeared. Now visitors, when they come, approach from the back along a thin ribbon of gravel driveway that cuts across a cornfield from modern Route 20.

The house has stood perched on the hilltop since the 1790s, surrounded on all sides by hundreds of acres of cultivated land. On the edge of the fields looms the remains of a forest that was once part of a larger, forbidding region known as the Wilderness. The house stood as an oasis in the middle of a dark, close wood.

In all the centuries it stood there, just two families ever owned the house. Many other families lived on the plantation, too—black families—but as property, not as owners.

They have all passed into the history of this place.

The trace of the old carriage lane still leads up the hill to Ellwood's front door.

The old catalpa tree that once grew in front of the house made it into the twenty-first century before it, too, finally passed into history. A seedling from that tree now grows in its place, and two other catalpas flank the old carriage entrance. There are maples and cedars and sycamores and a quartet of Kentucky coffee trees. The wind rustles their leaves. Birds chirp in their branches. They might be the only sounds on some days.

A recreated V Corps flag still hangs from the porch of Ellwood to commemorate the house's former use as Maj. Gen. Gouverneur Warren's headquarters. (cm)

On others, visitors can climb the front steps—sending the skink scurrying for the safety of its lair in one of the cracks between the stones—and go inside. Boot heels clunk on the wooden floors and echo off the walls.

There's the sound of friendly chatter. The sound of memories.

The sound of stories being told.

OPPOSITE: **The grounds of Ellwood provide plenty to see and explore. "Wildness" in many forms still encroaches on the well-tended property.** (cm)

CHAPTER ONE
1788-1863

They paid £30 a year to live in the middle of the wide, wild woods—an area *so* wild it had earned the name "the Wilderness." It was the Virginia frontier.

William and Betty Jones had come there to the edge of Spotsylvania County, in part, because the colony's most desirable land, along the Virginia Tidewater, had all been gobbled up. The interior of the colony, while perhaps not quite so inviting, at least offered the hope of better things to come. Pioneers had trickled into the region as early as 1714, when then-Governor Alexander Spotswood actively cultivated settlement, but the population remained sparse. The Wilderness, as a place to live, had never really caught on.

But sometime in the early 1770s, William and Betty, along with William's brother and sister-in-law, Churchill and Judith, separated themselves from their wealthy Tidewater family and moved to the Wilderness to live on land leased from Spotswood's heirs. The four toiled and tilled and made lives for themselves until, in 1788, William had collected enough to buy a chunk of property outright—£600 for 642 acres. Churchill, who had gone off to serve in the Continental Army, returned from the Revolution to set up a home, Woodville, on an adjoining parcel. The two brothers dined together four nights a week until Churchill's death in 1822.

By the mid-1790s, William began work on a two-story frame house that sat atop a long ridge overlooking the Wilderness Run valley. He called the house Ellwood, although the name also shows up in various records as "Elwood" and "Elkwood." The house served as the hub of a successful agricultural operation that grew corn, wheat, and oats. The property also boasted stables, barns,

The interior of Ellwood has undergone extensive renovation over the last 20 years; exhibits in the house explain that ongoing process. Although no evidence has been found that wallpaper was ever used in the house, the NPS says "wallpaper was common in mid-19th century homes of similar size and stature. The patterns displayed today are reproductions of those common to the period." (cm)

William Jones (left) and his daughter, Betty Churchill Jones (right). Betty was Jones's daughter from a second marriage, named after his first wife. (fsnmp)(fsnmp)

an outdoor kitchen, and cabins to house the 100 slaves who worked the land. A small family cemetery stood a few hundred yards south of the house. Several venerable trees graced the dooryard.

Over time, Jones became one of the wealthiest men in the county. Aside from the money he made from his agricultural holdings, he collected income from timber he sold as fuel to the local iron furnaces and collected rent from the Wilderness Tavern, which he built near the edge of his property along the turnpike that ran between Fredericksburg and Orange Court House.

Jones also added to his wealth by adding to his property, acquiring tracts of 100 acres, 253 acres, 910 acres. By 1830, the entire Ellwood plantation totaled 5,000 acres, worth $17,878. Compared to other antebellum plantations, Ellwood was pretty typical; compared to other homesteads scattered throughout the Wilderness, though, Ellwood seemed huge. The 400 acres of cleared, cultivated land—identified as "improved" land on the tax rolls—was four times larger than the Southern average for the time.

As one of the most prominent estates between Fredericksburg and Orange Court House, Ellwood frequently hosted guests. Revolutionary War hero "Light Horse" Harry Lee— father of Confederate Gen. Robert E. Lee—supposedly stayed in one of the upstairs rooms and wrote his memoirs. Another hero of the Revolution, the Marquis de Lafayette, dined at the house during his 1825 tour of America. Presidents James Madison and James Monroe may have also visited the house.

In 1823, on a trip to Richmond, Betty Jones died. Five years later, the 78-year-old Jones married 16-year-old Lucinda Gordon, his first wife's grandniece. In 1829, they had a daughter, whom they named Betty Churchill after Jones's first wife.

When Jones died in 1845, Lucinda inherited Ellwood—but only for the duration of her widowhood. If she remarried, she had to forfeit her claim on the estate, which she did in 1847. The following year, she

"The slave community at Ellwood included men and women with many skills," explains an NPS exhibit in the home. "Some, of course, simply worked the fields. But the workforce here also included carpenters, blacksmiths, cooks, and groomsmen. On the inventory of William Jones's estate, compiled after his death, they are all starkly lumped together—nickname, value, and occasional notes on their disabilities." (cm)

moved to her new husband's home, Greenwood, in Orange County, and her daughter, Betty, took formal possession of Ellwood.

That same year, Betty married J. Horace Lacy, a lawyer and educator. Lacy was "broken down aristocracy," said one local resident, fine looking and with a good education but no funds. Betty, a haughty woman who reportedly said she'd prefer to see the Devil walk up to her gate rather than a poor person, married Lacy anyway. "[A]fter he married her," said the local, "he became the lion of the Wilderness." The Lacys would eventually have eight children spaced over 17 years.

In 1857, the Lacys bought a grand manor in Fredericksburg called Chatham, which sat atop the bluffs overlooking the Rappahannock River. Chatham had once belonged to Betty's uncle, Churchill, and her father, William, but despite the family connection, their enthusiasm for the move, said Horace, was "softened down a little now by the thought that we must leave dear old Ellwood."

The Lacys did hold on to Ellwood, though, using it as a summer home, and life there continued much as it always had: till, plant, tend, and harvest. The goods were then shipped east to Fredericksburg and sold at market.

But in 1861, war rumbled across Virginia. Lacy, an ardent secessionist, joined the Confederate army, eventually working his way up to major. Betty, meanwhile, moved with her four children into the home of a friend in Fredericksburg. At Ellwood, operations continued under the supervision of a Mr. Jones—no relation to Betty's father—and a "skeleton force of slaves." Lacy had sent most of his slaves to a plantation he rented near the James River hoping the location, far removed from the fighting, would keep them secure.

At first, war only brushed Ellwood: a minor skirmish in late April 1863 as Confederates tried to delay the Union army's advance toward Chancellorsville. When the battle erupted, though, and wounded soldiers flooded to the rear, Ellwood became a field hospital. Shortly thereafter, Jones took Lacy's remaining slaves to the James River plantation, leaving Ellwood deserted.

In November, the two armies moved back into the area and faced off along Mine Run, seven miles to the west of Ellwood. As the Federal army marched by the plantation, soldiers ransacked the house, targeting, in particular, Lacy's library.

Nevertheless, Ellwood managed to weather these disruptions—troubles that would prove mild compared to what the war had yet to bring.

James Horace Lacy, whose portrait hangs in the second floor of Ellwood, had the bearing of an aristocrat without the bank account of one. His marriage to the wealthy Betty Churchill Jones changed everything for him. His financial influence, combined with his fierce firebrand attitudes, earned him the moniker "the most dangerous man in the Confederacy" in the early days of secession because he had the wealth and connections to push his political agenda. (cm)

At Ellwood

The trace of Ellwood's former driveway, which circled down to the Parker's Road Store, is still visible in front of the house. (cm)

The former Lacy house, Ellwood, is open seasonally, operated through an agreement with the National Park Service by the Friends of the Wilderness Battlefield. One of the house's downstairs rooms has been restored to look much as it might have when V Corps commander Gouverneur K. Warren used it as his headquarters. Other rooms feature interactive exhibits and displays that explain the battle, daily life in the house and on the plantation, and the restoration process that brought the house back to life from near ruin.

Outside, a 1.4-mile round trip walking path leads down to the old Parker's Store Road trace and, from there, to the original roadbed of the Orange Turnpike. Along the way, the path crosses Wilderness Run, which "served as Ellwood plantation's lifeblood," according to the N.P.S. "The run supplied water to the plantation since its earliest days. . . ." From here, Wilderness Run winds northward to eventually empty into the Rapidan River.

On the far side of the stream, the walking path leads to the former site of the Wilderness Tavern. Once, a tavern and several outbuildings occupied the area, although by the time of the battle, the tavern was no longer being used as such. The property was owned by 36-year-old William M. Simms, who who lived there with his family on 200 acres of land. The main house was located where the roadbed of modern Route 3 now runs. The ruins that remain on the property had been part of one of the dependencies, a one-and-a-half-story wood building that burned down in 1978. During part of the battle, Ambrose Burnside made his headquarters there.

From this location, a reporter from the *Boston Journal*, traveling with the Army of the Potomac, offered readers a look at the positions of each army as they prepared to square off:

> *Before the contest begins, go with me up to the old Wilderness tavern, which stands on the . . . plank road, and take a view of a portion of the battlefield. It will be a limited view, for there are few open spaces in the Wilderness.*
>
> *From the old tavern you look west. At your feet is a brook, flowing from the southwest, and another smaller stream from the northwest, joining their waters at the crossing*

of the turnpike and the plank road. The turnpike rises over a ridge between the two streams. On the south slope is the house of Major Lacy, owner of a house at Falmouth [Chatham], used by our forces after the battle of Fredericksburg. It is a beautiful view. A smooth lawn in front of the house, meadows green with the verdure of spring; beyond the meadows are hills thickly wooded, tall oaks and pine and cedar thickets. On the right hand side of the turnpike the ridge is more broken, and also thickly set with small trees and bushes. A mile and a half out from the crossing of the two roads the ridge breaks down into a ravine. Gen Lee has possession of the western bank, Grant the eastern. It is such a mixture of woods, underbrush, thickets, ravines, hills, hollows, knolls, that one is bewildered in passing through it, and to describe it a complete bewilderment to writer and reader.

Ellwood as seen from the Wilderness Tavern along the Orange Turnpike. (loc)

Across Route 3 from the site of the Wilderness Tavern is the site where Confederate surgeons set up a field hospital during the battle of Chancellorsville. It was there where Lt. Gen. Thomas "Stonewall" Jackson had his arm amputated. His chaplain, Rev. Beverly Tucker Lacy, took Jackson's amputated arm to Ellwood for burial because the chaplain's brother, James Horace Lacy, owned the plantation. Jackson's arm was interred in the family cemetery, which visitors today can still visit. A path leads down to the cemetery through rows of boxwoods and down to a field, where the cemetery rests beneath tall cedars.

During a rare quiet moment during the battle of the Wilderness, probably sometime on May 7, an engineering officer from New York, Wesley Brainerd, spent some time walking the grounds at Ellwood.

I was much interested and impressed on approaching a common looking farm house situated in an opening in the woods, to learn that Stonewall Jackson was buried near by.

James Horace Lacy's brother, Rev. Beverly Tucker Lacy, served as Stonewall Jackson's chaplain. Rev. Lacy's role in preserving Jackson's amputated arm has ensured his place in one of the Civil War's most unusual stories. (cm)

James Power Smith, one of Stonewall Jackson's most trusted staff officers, married into the Lacy family after the war. He erected a monument in the family cemetery to honor his former commander's amputated limb, buried there: "Arm of Stonewall Jackson." (cm)

His grave was situated in the heart of the Wilderness on a knoll, unmarked by stone or board. It was hard to realize, as I stood beside that lonely grave, that the little mound of earth before me hid from view all that was mortal of the man whose great deeds had filled the world with wonder and amazement. . . . I lingered for a long time at the grave of that wonderful and eccentric man.

Nor could I leave the spot without having experienced those peculiar feelings of awe and respect for the memory of the genius which, though that of an enemy, possessed the faculty which inspired his Soldiers with a religious enthusiasm, resulting in most wonderful victories and made his name a terror to ourselves.

The Union officer incorrectly believed that Jackson himself was buried at Ellwood, but in fact, only Jackson's arm had been interred there following its amputation.

The general himself lay buried miles away, near his home in Lexington, Virginia. Nevertheless, the arm, now marked by a small monument erected in 1903, evokes Jackson's presence, and even today it remains a point of interest for those who visit the property.

A path through boxwood trees once led visitors from Ellwood's gardens down to the site of the family cemetery, where Stonewall Jackson's arm is buried. (cm)

➤ TO STOP 2

From the end of Ellwood's driveway, turn right onto Route 20. Exercise caution, as the road can be busy. Travel 0.6 miles to the intersection with Route 3 and turn left at the light. Follow Route 3 West for 4.5 miles, then turn left onto the campus of Germanna Community College. Follow the campus drive 0.1 miles and turn right into the parking lot for the Germanna Visitor Center.

As you travel, note a couple landmarks: Past the light 0.3 miles, you will pass a parcel on the right marked by an old stone silo; that property had been the focus of a development controversy involving the so-called "Wilderness Walmart" (see next chapter). 3.5 miles past the parcel, you will pass the final location of the Walmart. The driveway for Germanna Community College is 0.7 miles past the Walmart on the left.

GPS: N 38.37768, W 77.78359

The Wilderness

CHAPTER TWO
1864

For 70 square miles, the undulating hills were awash in trees—"a vast sea" of dense forest, wrote one visitor.

Another described the region less kindly as "one of the waste places of nature." "It is a region of gloom and the shadow of death," said another. Someone even likened it to "the wildest regions of Dante's 'Inferno.'"

This was the Wilderness, a thick second-growth forest that sprawled across the rolling terrain of central Virginia. The hills themselves, like choppy waves, rose and fell and broke in all directions. The forest, thick and vibrant, laid claim to everything else.

It was young, as forests go. Once, magnificent stands of timber grew on the hills. But settlers found iron ore, abundant in the region, in the early 1700s. By 1718, the first of several iron furnaces opened to smelt the ore and process it for export. Those furnaces, of course, needed fuel; some could burn as much as 750 acres's worth of timber in a year. To provide that fuel, furnace owners clear-cut much of the region's trees.

In the wake of that clear-cutting, a second-growth forest sprung up—a dense growth of scrubby pines and whiplash oaks, briars and thorn bushes, vines and ivies and creepers, honeysuckle, and wild roses. "You had a tangle through which a dog could hardly force its way," said one man.

A few streams wound their way among the hills, and the depressions in the terrain hid wet, marshy spots. "The scrawny, moss-tagged pines, the garroted alders, the hoary willows," said one visitor, "gives a very sad look to these wet thickets."

A macadamized turnpike ran through the heart of the Wilderness, stretching east toward Fredericksburg

Sunlight remains a premium in "the dark, close wood," which is a much more mature forest now than it was in the 1860s. The high tree canopy blocks out light, making it harder for ground cover to grow. That means the forest today is much more open than it was at the time of the battle. (cm)

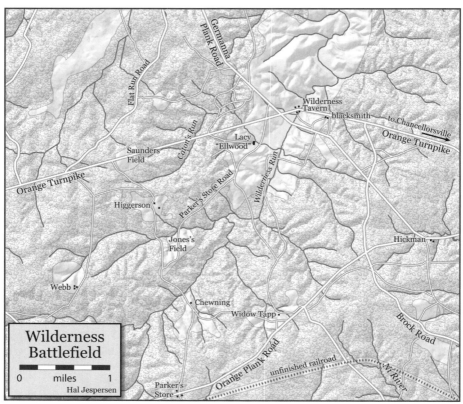

WILDERNESS BATTLEFIELD—Described by one combatant as "one of the waste places of nature," the Wilderness consisted of 70 square miles of second-growth forest. Looking at it on the map, Ulysses S. Grant recognized it as a topographical obstacle and wanted George Gordon Meade to move the Army of the Potomac through as quickly as possible. Robert E. Lee saw the Wilderness not as an obstacle but an opportunity; the forest and terrain would negate much of the Federal army's numerical superiority.

and west toward Orange Court House. A second road, the Orange Plank Road, which got its name from the timber planks used as paving, also twisted through the area. Few other good roads traversed the region, "only a labyrinth of wagon tracks and bridle paths leading to and from the river to the furnaces and clearings of the settlers," according to one traveler.

Indeed, as inhospitable as the Wilderness seemed, a few families eked out livings by farming small patches cut out of the forest. Some owned slaves, although many were too poor.

Residents had a store, Parker's Store, which sat along the Orange Plank Road. To meet their spiritual needs, they had the Wilderness Church, first built along Orange Turnpike around 1778 and rebuilt in 1853. A few miles to the west of the church sat the Wilderness Tavern, where the stagecoach stopped. Travelers

A correspondent from the *Philadelphia Inquirer* described the Wilderness in an article widely reproduced across the north:

The word wilderness conveys generally the impression of a deserted waste; and the term, applied to the region in which the great battle was fought, was no misnomer. It is an exceedingly broken table land, irregular in its confirmation and so densely covered with dwarf timber and undergrowth, as to render progress through it very difficult and laborious off the few roads and paths that penetrate it. The timber was so effectually [an ally] of the rebels, for they had taken care to take position near its edge, leaving us an open country at our back, so that a whole division drawn up in battle might be invisible a few hundred feet off. (cm)

heading southwest toward Orange Court House could also stop at Robertson's Tavern or, if heading south toward Spotsylvania Court House, at Todd's Tavern. If heading east toward Fredericksburg, travelers could seek lodging at the tavern at the Chancellorsville crossroads.

In the spring of 1863, war swept through the Wilderness. The Army of the Potomac, in an attempt to slip behind the Confederate Army of Northern Virginia, which was hunkered down in a nearly impregnable position in Fredericksburg some 12 miles to the east, marched into the Wilderness from the north and west. The Confederates discovered the Federal maneuver in time and intercepted the larger army just as it was forging eastward from Chancellorsville. The resulting battle left 30,000 casualties in its wake. Many who died were buried where they fell—or never buried at all.

The Wilderness Tavern offered one of the few oases in the middle of the wild. (fsnmp)

When the armies again converged on the Wilderness a year later, the forest gave up those dead. Union soldiers, camping near the Chancellorsville intersection, found the bones of fallen comrades washed out of their shallow graves or dug up by wild animals. "The dead horses had dwindled away to bones and the dead men to bones and underclothing," wrote one soldier. "I found a dozen skulls in twice as many rods travel and could doubtless have found scores by a little examination of the thick underbrush."

"This, viewed as a battleground, was simply infernal," a Union soldier later said.

The thick foliage of the Wilderness made the country nearly impenetrable. There was little room for cavalry to operate, artillery to deploy, or large bodies of men to maneuver. "It is impossible to conceive a field worse adapted to the movements of a grand army," wrote a Union officer. "A more unpromising theatre of war was never seen," said another.

The modern Wilderness Church sits near the location of the original church built in 1778. (cm)

Lieutenant General Ulysses S. Grant, commander of all Union armies, saw the Wilderness as a formidable obstacle that stood between the Army of the Potomac and the Army of Northern Virginia. The ground offered no possibility for drawing Lee's army out into open combat. "All the conditions were favorable for defensive operations," Grant noted.

Grant had almost 119,000 men at his disposal, and although he didn't know Lee's strength—the Confederates had 66,000 men available—Grant felt confident in his numerical superiority. "[I]t was my intention to fight Lee between Culpeper and Richmond if he would stand," Grant later wrote.

But first, the Army of the Potomac had to get through the Wilderness as quickly as possible and into the open country beyond. Only then could Grant bring his numerical superiority to bear.

The Army of the Potomac breaks camp around Culpeper in preparation for the spring campaign of 1864. (fsnmp)

And so, beginning on May 3, 1864, the Union army began to thaw after its long winter of dormancy. "We were all up by starlight; a warm, clear night," wrote one army staff officer, Theodore Lyman; "had our breakfast by daybreak, and at 5:25 a.m. turned our back on our little village of the last six months and the grove about it, dear even its desolation!"

Roads, like dry riverbeds, suddenly filled with a rush of blue as the Army of the Potomac flowed south, over the Rapidan River and into the heart of the most inhospitable terrain the army had ever occupied.

The Wilderness, unruly, interminable, and still haunted by the failures of the previous year, pressed in on all sides. "It was," said Horace Porter, one of Grant's closest aides, "a wilderness in the most forbidding sense of the word."

At Germanna Ford

As one wing of the Federal army moved eastward from Culpeper toward Orange County, engineers constructed two bridges across the Rapidan River to facilitate the army's crossing. One span crossed where the westbound lane of the current highway bridge spans the river; the second crossed just downriver of the first. "There were two pontoons," recalled Theodore Lyman, one of Meade's aides, "a wooden one & a canvass, the ascent up the opposite high & steep bank was bad, with a difficult turn at the top."

The crossing "took a good deal of time because of the delay in getting them up the steep ascent. Sat on the bank and watched the steady stream, as it came over. That eve took a bath in the Rapid Ann and thought that might come sometimes to bathe in the James!"

After they crossed, the army halted where they camped the night of their withdrawal from Mine Run the previous December. "*Sapristi*, it was cold that night!" Lyman recalled. "Though here was green grass in place of an half inch of ice . . ."

A path leads from the parking lot of Germanna Foundation's visitor center and museum, along the eastbound lane of Route 3, down to a modern canoe launch located on the south side of the bridge. The area is not generally accessible to the public.

Behind the visitor center stands a memorial to the original settlers of the Germanna colony. Stone tablets outline the history of the settlement, which dates back to 1714.

The surrounding memorial garden serves as the final

The Union army built two bridges to facilitate its crossing at Germanna Ford. Relative to the camera angle in the above photo, which was taken from the river's south bank, the modern Germanna Visitors Center sits slightly behind and to the right. (loc)

The five-sided Brawdus Martin Germanna Visitors Center is open each week on a limited basis. Check its website for hours: http://germanna.org/about/visitor-center/. (cm)

resting place for Col. John Spotswood, the son of former Governor Alexander and Lady Spotswood, who had grown up at Germanna and later served the Episcopal parish in Fredericksburg in the 1750s. An obelisk at the center of the garden marks his grave.

Located half a mile east of Germanna—situated on the north side of Route 3—sits a Walmart that had once been at the center of a major preservation battle that attracted national attention. In 2008, the retail giant announced plans for a new 138,000-square-foot superstore near the intersection of Routes 3 and 20—3.5 miles east of the current location on the same side of Route 3. While no fighting took place on the spot where Walmart intended to build, it did serve as a vital part of the Union army's logistics hub.

A state historic marker recounting Orange County's rich history sits adjacent to historically significant property that, ironically, Orange County once green-lighted to Walmart for development. (cm)

For three years, preservationists, county officials, Walmart, and local residents went round and round over the plans. In January 2011, just when it appeared Wal-Mart was finally able to move forward with construction, the retailer announced it would preserve the property and build farther down the road. "We firmly believe that preservation and progress need not be mutually exclusive, and welcome Walmart as a thoughtful partner in efforts to protect the Wilderness Battlefield," Civil War Trust President O. James Lighthizer said at the time.

In November of 2013, the company turned the property over to the Commonwealth of Virginia for perpetual preservation. "This is a wonderful legacy gift from Wal-Mart that comes during the mid-point of the Sesquicentennial of the Civil War," said Kathleen S. Kilpatrick, director of the Department of Historic Resources. "We look forward to working with community leaders to steward the property and realize its potential for public benefit."

As though to underscore its commitment to history, Walmart installed a series of signs in front of its Route 3 store highlighting Orange County's colorful past—Civil War and otherwise. (cm)

The grave of Col. John Spotswood, son of former Virginia Gov. Alexander Spotswood, for whom Spotsylvania County is named for. The suffix *–sylvania* means "forest land," so Spotsylvania literally translates to "Spots forest land" or "Spotswoods." The Spotswood grave sits at the center of a memorial garden behind the Germanna Visitors Center.

➤ TO STOP 3

Exit the parking lot by turning right onto the campus drive. Travel 0.1 miles to the intersection with Route 3. Turn right onto Route 3 East and travel 4.5 miles back to the intersection with Route 20. At the light, turn right and travel 0.4 miles. The pull-off for Grant's Headquarters is on the right.

GPS: N 38.32227, W 77.73395

Grant Takes Command

CHAPTER THREE

The pile of wood shavings at his feet had grown steadily throughout the afternoon.

Across the Orange Turnpike, next to the Lacy house, Union artillery maintained a near-constant barrage aimed at the Confederates somewhere farther to the west. Somewhere else, the muffled sound of rifle fire tried to push its way through thick underbrush. Couriers raced into headquarters on horseback, delivered the scribbled messages entrusted to their care, then raced away with fresh orders.

Ulysses S. Grant paid little heed to any of it. He hardly even paid attention to the penknife he held in his right glove as he sliced away strip after thin strip of wood from the stick he held in his left. When he worked one stick into shavings, he picked up another and started anew. The whittling, said an aide, played "sad havoc" on the gloves, which had several holes peeled into them.

"It was amusing," said an observer, "to see him—the Commander-in-Chief—whittling away with his knife upon the bark of a tree, pausing now and then to throw in a word or sentence in the conversation of those grouped about, and then going to work again with renewed vigor upon the incision of the pine."

The observer, a newspaper correspondent who had traveled with Grant in Mississippi and Tennessee, knew the general well. "[B]ut as I strolled thro' the group of officers reclining under the trees at headquarters, I looked for him some time in vain, such was his insignificant, unpretending aspect and conduct while the battle was raging in all its fury," the reporter admitted. He thought a stranger to headquarters "would have little dreamed that the plain, quiet man who sat with his back against

Heavily wooded now, there's little to see at Grant's headquarters, which sits just a few dozen feet away from busy Route 20. (cm)

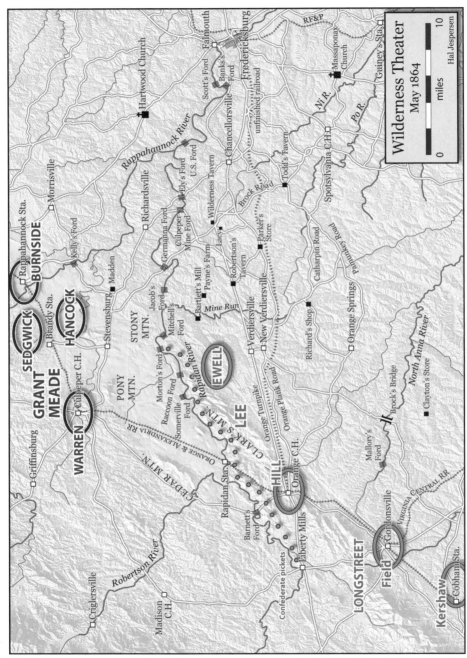

WILDERNESS THEATER— The Federals concentrated around Culpeper for the winter of 1863-64 while Lee spread his Confederates in a defensive arc along the Rapidan River. Longstreet's corps, stationed in Tennessee for much of the winter, arrived by train in Gordonsville in mid-April; Lee positioned them so they could shift eastward with the rest of the army or southward to protect Richmond, depending on how the spring campaign developed.

Grant whittled while the Wilderness burned. (loc)

a tree, apparently heedless and unmoved, was the one on whom the fortunes of the day, if not of the age and country, were hinging."

As he whittled, he smoked cigars. On bad days, like today, he might go through as many as 20 of them. If he felt particularly stressed, the puffs of smoke popped from the cigar's end more feverishly, more frequently, but otherwise, said the correspondent, Grant maintained an "imperturbability of countenance."

*   *   *

He had come from the West, this quiet, unassuming man, and he was unlike anything the Army of the Potomac had seen before. Some noted "a good deal of rough-looking dignity" in the new lieutenant general, but overall, "there was no enthusiasm shown by the men on the arrival of their new commander."

"[H]e rode along the line in a slouchy unobservant way," one artillerist recounted after getting a look at Grant in late April, "with his coat unbuttoned and setting anything but an example of military bearing to the troops. . . ." They were used to the showiness of George McClellan, the good-natured but martial appearance of Ambrose Burnside, the hard-edged bluster of "Fighting Joe" Hooker, the booming temper of George Gordon Meade. "[Grant] is by no means a handsome man and

"All the newspaper reports about the immense enthusiasm for him are bosh . . ." an artillerist noted dismissively of U.S. Grant, who elicited ambivalence from the Army of the Potomac, despite the media's love affair with the commander: "[T]here seems to be a determination now to find no fault with Grant."(loc)

alongside of Burnside looks like 'small potatoes,'" an IX Corps soldier confided in a letter to his family back home. Another described him as "stumpy, unmilitary, slouchy, and Western-looking; very ordinary in fact."

"There is no enthusiasm in the army for Gen. Grant," reiterated Col. Seldon Conner of the 19th Maine; "and, on the other hand, there is no prejudice against him. We are prepared to throw up our hats for him when he shows himself the great soldier here in Virginia against Lee and the best troops of the rebels." Grant's reputation as "the great soldier" out west held little sway with the men of the Army of the Potomac. "Well, Grant has never met Bobby Lee yet," they said to each other.

Yet none of them could deny that Grant had won important victories at Forts Henry and Donelson and at Shiloh. In a fit of jealousy over the successes, his own superior, Maj. Gen. Henry Halleck, tried to retire him, but President Lincoln himself recalled Grant from exile. "I can't spare this man," Lincoln reportedly said. "He fights." Grant repaid the president's confidence by winning a crucial victory at Vicksburg and then crossing Tennessee to save the Union army trapped in Chattanooga.

"Grant is emphatically an executive man, whose only place is in the field," said Army of the Potomac commander Maj. Gen. George Gordon Meade after first meeting the new lieutenant general. "God knows I shall hail his advent with delight if it results in carrying on operations in the manner I have always desired," he wrote in another letter to his wife. "Cheerfully will I give him all credit if he can bring the war to a close." (loc)

In the East, meanwhile, the Army of the Potomac had achieved a major victory at Gettysburg, but the army commander, Maj. Gen. George Gordon Meade, let the Confederates escape without a vigorous pursuit. In the months afterward, Meade's greatest success may have been that he hadn't lost a major engagement—but he hadn't managed to be in one, either. Like his predecessors, Meade seemed content to avoid a pitched battle with Lee.

So Lincoln brought Grant east.

Lincoln didn't want Grant to command just a single army, though. Instead, he promoted Grant to lieutenant general—a rank not permanently awarded to a U.S. military commander since George Washington—and he placed Grant in charge of all Federal armies. "You are vigilant and self-reliant," Lincoln told him; "and, pleased with this, I wish not to obtrude any constraints or restraints upon you."

Lincoln believed he had finally found a general who understood the grim math of war and who possessed the resolve to do what needed to be done, as unpleasant as it would be.

And perhaps Grant did. "He habitually wears an expression as if he had determined to drive his head through a brick wall, and was about to do it," a staff officer with the Army of the Potomac noted with admiration shortly after Grant's promotion. "I have much confidence in him."

Grant believed no peace could be possible with the South "until the military power of the rebellion was

Executive Mansion
Washington, April 30. 1864.

Lieutenant General Grant:

Not expecting to see you again before the Spring campaign opens, I wish to express, in this way, my entire satisfaction with what you have done up to this time, so far as I understand it. The particulars of your plans I neither know, or seek to know. You are vigilant and self-reliant; and, pleased with this, I wish not to obtrude any constraints or restraints upon you. While I am very anxious that any great disaster, or the capture of our men in great numbers, shall be avoided, I know these points are less likely to escape your attention than they would be mine. If there is anything wanting which is within my power to give, do not fail, to let me know it. And now with a brave Army, and a just cause, may God sustain you.

Yours very truly
A. Lincoln.

Abraham Lincoln's letter to Ulysses S. Grant, April 30, 1864. (hl)

entirely broken." So far, the Confederacy had thwarted Federal attempts at breaking that military power despite the fact that "the resources of the enemy and his numerical strength were far inferior to ours."

The answer, Grant believed, was "to hammer continuously against the armed force of the enemy and his resources, until by mere attrition, if in no other way, there should be nothing left to him. . . ."

To achieve this, Grant developed a grand strategy that would mobilize all Federal armies in concert with one another —something never before attempted during the war. The coordinated movement would allow him "to use the greatest number of troops practicable against the armed forces of the enemy, preventing him from using the same force at different seasons against first one and then another of our armies. . . ."

He ordered his friend and confidant, Maj. Gen.

As he marched into the Wilderness, George F. Williams of the 146th New York infantry recalled seeing the Union army's commanders standing in a nook in the woods along the roadside:

General Meade was standing on the bank that overlooked the road, his soldierly figure contrasting strangely with that of the lieutenant-general, who was seated on a decaying stump, apparently more interested in the toe of his boot than our movements. An unlighted cigar was between Grant's teeth, and he chewed his weed viciously. When our regiment came in front of the two generals, I caught a glimpse of General Grant's eyes, as he lifted them for a moment. Clear and steady, calm and confident, this great leader seemed in that single glance to take in the face of every man within his range; and I was impressed by the strong will betokened by the square chin and the firm mouth of the man who was planning and conducting our campaign. The tall, courtly figure of Meade, his trim gray hair, and neat regulation cap, gave him a martial look, as he leaned on his saber; while the heavy frame of Grant, who wore no sword, seemed the very opposite of my preconceived ideas of our new commander. The wide-brimmed hat, pulled down over his eyes, and the closely clipped beard, made the renowned chieftain appear so unlike a soldier that it needed the uniform and the broad shoulder-strap, with its row of triple stars, to remind one that here was a warrior already famous. (fsnmp)

William Tecumseh Sherman, to move south from Tennessee toward Atlanta, Georgia. He ordered Maj. Gen. Nathaniel Banks to move from New Orleans toward Mobile, Alabama. In Virginia, he ordered Maj. Gen. Franz Sigel to move up the Shenandoah Valley and Maj. Gen. Benjamin Butler to move up the Peninsula toward Richmond.

Meade, meanwhile, was to take the Army of the Potomac and engage Lee's Army of Northern Virginia. "Lee's army will be your objective," Grant told Meade. "Wherever Lee goes, there you will go also."

And Grant, too, would go. He announced his intention to make his office not back in Washington but in the field with Meade's army. In deference, Meade offered to resign, but Grant assured him his services were needed. Grant planned to tell Meade what he wanted done and leave it to Meade to figure out the best way to execute those wishes.

Meade was pleased. "[Grant] is so much more

active than his predecessor, and agrees so well with me in his views, I cannot but be rejoiced at his arrival, because I believe success to be the more probable," he later wrote to his wife. "My duty is plain, to continue quietly to discharge my duties, heartily co-operating with him and under him."

* * *

Grant and Meade launched their offensive against Lee by sending forward elements of the army across the Rapidan River on May 3, 1864. The rest of the army followed on May 4, crossing at Germanna Ford and Ely's Ford, using the two roads to prevent bottlenecking their large force. The maneuver also gave them flexibility. No one was quite sure how Lee might react—or even where, exactly, Lee was—so the parallel approaches across the river gave the army the option of several routes to get at the Confederates.

As soon as Grant got word that Confederates were nearby, he scribbled orders to pitch into them immediately. (loc)

If Lee moved into his former position behind Mine Run, Grant intended to swing south of the creek and outflank his position. On the other hand, if Lee fell back toward Richmond, Grant would be in position to overtake the Confederates and force them to fight in open country, where he had little doubt his much larger army would prevail. No one in the Union high command seemed to seriously consider the possibility that Lee might attack them in the Wilderness.

When Lee did strike, then, on May 5, it sent part of the Federal command into near panic. What other tricks did the Confederate commander have up his gold-braided sleeve, they fretted.

"I am heartily tired of hearing what Lee is going to do," Grant finally snapped after a day and a half of battle. "Some of you always seem to think he is suddenly going to turn a double somersault, and land on our rear and on both our flanks at the same time. Go back to your command, and try to think what we are going to do ourselves, instead of what Lee is going to do."

Accurate information on that first morning, May 5, proved hard to come by for Grant and Meade both. Union cavalry failed to properly scout out the Confederate position. Union corps commanders couldn't get a clear picture of the events unfolding right in front of them.

The entire Federal army was strung out along the road for miles. And gray-clad troops poured and poured down one road, then another, filling the woods between.

The situation might have daunted a different man, but Grant, itching for a fight with Lee, issued a decisive command to Meade: "If any opportunity presents itself of pitching into a part of Lee's army, do so without giving time for disposition." This, like Grant's approach to nearly everything else, represented a markedly different way of thinking for the Army of the Potomac. Lee always preferred to take the initiative, and former Federal commanders had always seemed to oblige him. Grant refused to let his army dance to Lee's tune any longer.

"No movement of the enemy seemed to puzzle or disconcert him," said a correspondent. At one point, on the second day of battle, Confederate artillery fire swept close to Grant's headquarters. "General," said an officer, "wouldn't it be prudent to move headquarters . . . until the result of the present attack is known?" Grant puffed his cigar. "It strikes me," he replied, "that it would be better to order up some artillery and defend the present location."

It was classic Grant. After the first day at Shiloh, when the surprise Confederate attack had nearly driven Grant's army into the river, a near-despairing Sherman found his commander under a tree with a cigar. "Well, Grant," Sherman said, "we've had the devil's own day of it, haven't we?" "Yes," Grant replied. "Lick 'em tomorrow, though." And he did.

But despite his cool demeanor, Grant fully felt the weight of the responsibility he bore. On the evening of May 6, after the final threat of the day had been repulsed, after two days of unprecedented battlefield carnage, Grant gave up his whittling and his cigar smoking and retired to his tent. His chief of staff, Brig. Gen. John Rawlins, later said he "had never before seen [Grant] show the slightest apprehension or sense of danger; but on that memorable night in the Wilderness it was much more than personal danger which confronted him. No one knew better than he that he was face to face with destiny, and there was no doubt that he realized it fully and understood perfectly that retreat from that field meant a great calamity to his country as well as to himself."

There in his tent, Rawlins said, face down on his cot, Grant "gave vent to his feelings in a way which left no room to doubt that he was deeply moved."

The battle had whittled away his calm exterior at last.

But Grant's resolve remained. The general emerged from his tent a short time later to sit by the fire, stone faced, mulling his options.

He was ready to make another go at the Confederates, ready to try again to lick 'em tomorrow.

At Grant's Headquarters

Today, there's little to see at or from Grant's knoll aside from forest and a pair of wayside signs. Visitors who stop to make the short walk to the site—a few hundred feet from the road—should exercise caution because traffic along Route 20—the old Orange Turnpike—can be heavy.

"Years ago a turnpike was built from Fredericksburg to Orange Court House . . ." wrote a reporter from the *Boston Journal*. "General Grant has established his headquarters at [a] crossing, his flag waving from a knoll west of the road. A mile and a half out on the turnpike, on a ridge . . . and there . . . I can see long lines of rebel infantry—the sunlight beaming from the bayonet and gun barrel.

Grant's aid, Horace Porter, described the headquarters knoll in greater detail:

[I]n the northwest angle formed by the two intersecting roads, was a knoll from which the old trees had been cut, and upon which was a second growth of scraggy pine, scrub-oak, and other timber. The knoll was high enough to afford a view for some little distance, but the outlook was limited in all directions by the almost impenetrable forest with its interlacing trees and tangled undergrowth.

In 2001 and again in 2007, the Central Virginia Battlefields Trust preserved tracts at Grant's Knoll totalling eighteen acres.

Motorists today tend to pass through the Wilderness rather than stop there, which had been Grant's plan, too, but when the Confederate army challenged him, he decided to fight. Visitors who stop at the site of Grant's headquarters should exercise extreme caution because Route 20 can be especially busy. (cm)

⟶ TO STOP 4A

Using extreme caution, merge onto Route 20 West and continue on in the direction you had been traveling. Continue for 1.3 miles, and pull into the parking lot for the Wilderness Exhibit Shelter, which will be on the right. Remain there for the next two chapters.

GPS: N 38.31825, W 77.75473

Lee Moves In

CHAPTER FOUR
MAY 5, 1864

All spring long, Robert E. Lee watched and worried. Much of his success as the commander of the Army of Northern Virginia had stemmed from his ability to take the measure of his opponent. It had allowed him to act with audacity, as when he turned, with his back to the Potomac, to challenge George McClellan at Antietam in September 1862, or when he divided his army not once but three times in front of a cowed "Fighting Joe" Hooker at Chancellorsville in May 1863. Now, in the spring of 1864, he faced a new Federal opponent: Lt. Gen. Ulysses S. Grant. While Lee didn't seem overly impressed at the news of Grant's appointment, he wasn't immediately sure what to make of Grant, either.

But Lee's trusted "Old Warhorse," Lt. Gen. James Longstreet, knew exactly what to make of the new Union commander. "That man will fight us every day and every hour till the end of the war," warned Longstreet, who knew Grant's temperament if anyone did: He and Grant had been friends in the pre-war army, and Longstreet had served as best man at Grant's wedding.

"It behooves us to be on the alert, or we will be deceived," Lee worried. "You know that is part of Grant's tactics." Lee even worried that press reports about Grant's plans had "an appearance of design . . . intended to mislead us as to the enemy's intention."

Every piece of intelligence that came to Lee during March and April gave him more to worry about. "[A] large number of recruits are being sent to the Army of the Potomac," said one informant, who "expressed surprize at the number of troops conveyed on the [railroad]." Every train, Lee told Confederate President Jefferson Davis, brings the Army of the Potomac new

"[T]he army of Genl Meade is in motion, and is crossing the Rapidan on our right, whether with the intention of attacking, or moving towards Fredericksburg, I am not able to say," Gen. Robert E. Lee wrote to Jefferson Davis on May 4. "But it is apparent that the long threatened effort to take Richmond has begun, and that the enemy has collected all his available force to accomplish it." (loc)

recruits. "Their clothes are too new & overcoats of too deep a blue for old troops," he reported to Richmond.

As he worried about the swelling numbers of the Federal army, Lee also worried about the uncertain number of men in his own army. Many had deserted over the winter because of a lack of supplies or their own proximity to home, although as the spring campaign season neared, many of the stragglers began to return to the ranks.

He had also detached a significant portion of his army—some 11,000 men under Longstreet—to special duty in Tennessee. Throughout March and into April, Lee prodded Longstreet to keep an eye on his front, and as soon as Longstreet felt comfortable that the Federals there had withdrawn, he was to return to Virginia as quickly as possible.

Lee was also concerned enough about manpower to issue a circular to his men: "I hope that few of the soldiers of this army will find it necessary at any time in the coming campaign to surrender themselves prisoners of war. We cannot spare brave men to fill Federal prisons."

Even as he worried about having enough men, he worried about how to feed and clothe them. "The great obstacle everywhere is scarcity of supplies," Lee told Longstreet. Conditions were tight enough that Lee's wife sent him weekly caches of socks to distribute to soldiers.

Still, conditions weren't as bad as they'd been the previous winter, noted Lee's chief of staff, Col. Walter Taylor. "Our army is in excellent condition in every way," he wrote. "Its morale is not to be surpassed—its sanitary condition was never so good—it is now well fed—and strange to relate is well and entirely shod. More could not be said in favor of any army that ever took the field."

By the time the campaign opened, Lee had some 66,000 men available to him, including Longstreet's corps. Overall, the army was slightly larger than it had been when he'd achieved his great victory at Chancellorsville the previous May. After that, as Lee moved north into Pennsylvania, the army's size swelled to 75,000—although Confederates took heavy casualties at the Battle of Gettysburg in early July. No one considered Gettysburg as anything other than a setback, though, and certainly no one looked at it as the "High Water Mark of the Confederacy" (a convenient conceit crafted by a marketing-savvy man named John Badger Bachelder who, in the 1890s, worked to promote Gettysburg as a tourism destination).

At the start of the Gettysburg Campaign in early June, Lee spent a night at Ellwood. Perhaps there, in the yard outside the house where his own father had written his memoirs, Lee reflected on his own fortunes of

war. Certainly, by the time he wrote to his wife when he reached Culpeper a few days later, he was in a ruminating mood. "The country here looks very green & pretty notwithstanding the ravages of war," Lee wrote. "[Y]ou must remember me in your prayers, & implore the Lord of Hosts for the removal of the terrible scourge with which He has thought best to afflict our bleeding country."

As summer stretched into fall, the morale of the army—and the Confederacy in general—remained high. "The Army of Northern Virginia alone, as the last hope of the South . . . will sooner or later by its own unaided power win the independence of the Confederacy," wrote a Georgia officer with unbridled confidence.

Throughout the fall, Lee, too, remained confident—if somewhat frustrated—as the armies tussled in a series of minor engagements and skirmishes. Although neither side scored any decisive victories, Lee successfully demonstrated his continued ability to parry movements by the much larger Federal army. The final confrontation of the campaign occurred along Mine Run, just seven miles west of the Wilderness, in the last days of November. The Union commander, George Gordon Meade, called off a planned assault at the last moment after getting a closer look at the strength of the Confederate fortifications. "If I had thought there was any reasonable degree of probability of success, I would have attacked," Meade wrote to his wife. "I did not think so; on the contrary, believed it would result it useless and criminal slaughter of brave men, and might result in serious disaster to the army. I determined not to attack, no other movements were practicable, and I withdrew."

The Federal army returned north of the Rapidan River, toward its supply bases around Culpeper Court House and Brandy Station, to spend the winter. "I am greatly disappointed at his getting off with so little damage," Lee admitted.

Lee kept his army south of the river, spreading

As the spring 1864 campaign season opened, Lee had been working with a three-corps command structure for nearly a year—with decidedly mixed results. Lt. Gen. James Longstreet commanded the First Corps; Lt. Gen. Richard Ewell the Second; and Lt. Gen. A. P. Hill the Third. (loc)(loc)(loc)

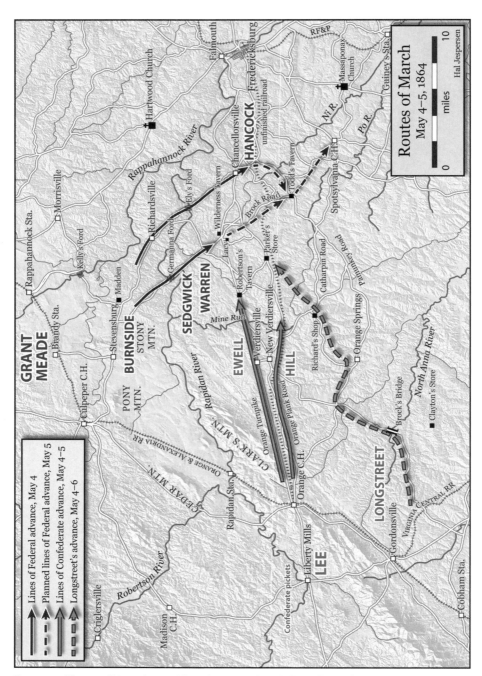

ROUTES OF MARCH—Attempting a wide swing around Lee's flank, Federals entered the Wilderness on May 4, 1864. Lee immediately moved to intercept them, sending his Second and Third Corps along parallel roads to strike the strung-out Federal column on May 5. The First Corps, posted in the rear, farthest from the Wilderness, cut cross-country to make it to the battle, arriving on the field on the morning of May 6.

out between Mine Run and Orange Court House, and prepared to weather the cold months. He knew spring would bring a renewed Federal offensive, and he watched from afar all winter long as the Federals prepared. Grant's appointment and subsequent decision to campaign with the Army of the Potomac added one more unknown element to the mix.

When Longstreet returned in mid-April, Lee held him in reserve near the rail junction of Gordonsville. That way, depending on the direction Grant eventually advanced, Lee could send Longstreet on one of several routes to help counter the Federal thrust. Ever aggressive and ever looking to grasp the initiative, Lee waited impatiently for Grant to make that first move, but he had no other choice. In the meantime, he prepared his army so it could respond when the time came. "If I am forced to retire from this line, either by a flank movement of the enemy or the want of supplies," Lee warned Davis, "great injury will befall us."

The troops could sense the building tension. "Everything indicates preparation for active service about the 1st of May," a Confederate surgeon wrote. "Genl. Grant's wings have to be clipped, and I think Genl. Lee can do him that honor."

Even Lee showed renewed vigor at the thought of battle. Taylor noted that "it really seemed to do him good to look forward to the trial of strength soon to ensue between himself and the present idol of the North."

Grant showed his hand on May 3 when advance elements of his army began to cross the Rapidan River, with the bulk of the army following on May 4. "[W]hether with the intention of attacking, or moving towards Fredericksburg, I am not able to say," Lee wrote to Davis. "But it is apparent that the long threatened effort to take Richmond has begun, and that the enemy has collected all his available force to accomplish it."

Lee had watched and worried long enough.

Rather than let the Federal movement play out further, Lee chose to seize the initiative. He pushed his army forward along two parallel roads, the Orange Turnpike and, just to its south, the Orange Plank Road, in the hope of catching the Federals on the march and off guard. The impenetrable Wilderness would make it difficult for Grant to respond effectively despite his superior numbers, thus nullifying Grant's greatest advantage.

"The troops are all in excellent spirits, and eager for the fray," said a South Carolinian. "Gen. Grant's glory will soon vanish away, and his great name buried along with those of his unfortunate predecessors."

"THE TROOPS ARE ALL IN EXCELLENT SPIRITS, AND EAGER FOR THE FRAY."

— *South Carolina Infantryman*

Quandary at Saunders' Field

CHAPTER FIVE
MAY 5, 1864

There was "something oppressive in the dim light and the strange quiet," a Union officer noted. He could not tell why, or where his feeling came from.

It was May 5, an hour after daybreak.

The Union army had already begun its march for the day, and although the narrow, forest-choked roads made movement difficult, everything seemed to be going relatively well. Major General Gouverneur Warren's V Corps led the march. A few miles behind him, near Germanna Ford, Maj. Gen. John Sedgwick's VI Corps followed. To the east, along Ely's Ford Road, Maj. Gen. Winfield Scott Hancock's II Corps traveled a parallel route. Still on the north side of the Rapidan River, Maj. Gen. Ambrose E. Burnside's IX Corps brought up the rear.

The wings of the army would move a little farther south, then swing westward to search out the Army of Northern Virginia and do battle. Somewhere out there they knew, miles beyond the Wilderness, the Confederates waited.

Nearly all of Warren's corps had passed beyond the Orange Turnpike, following a wagon road that skirted the Ellwood plantation and led to Parker's Store along the Orange Plank Road a few miles to the south. The rear guard, under Brig. Gen. Charles Griffin, prepared to pack up and join the rest of their corps, but then one of the pickets spotted something, like an early morning mirage, far down the road just before it dissolved into the horizon: horsemen in gray. The pickets watched as the horsemen drew closer—with gray-clad infantry marching behind them. "With the aide of my

The 140th New York, from the Rochester area, suffered 23 killed, 118 wounded, and 114 missing out of 529 men engaged. Reenactors representing the regiment dedicated a granite monument to the unit at a ceremony on May 7, 1989. (cm)(cm)

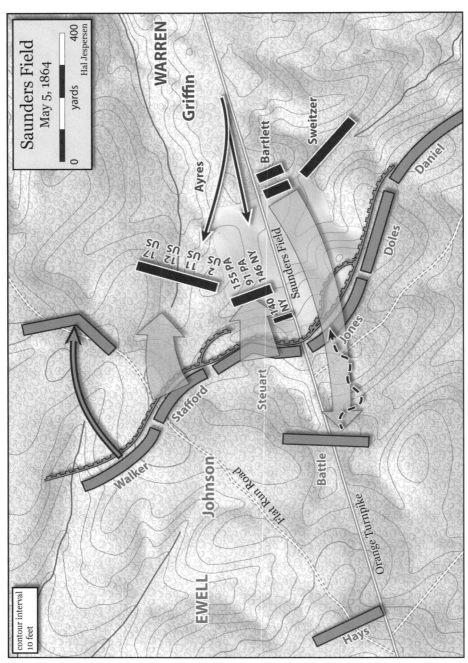

SAUNDERS FIELD—The topography of Saunders Field split Warren's assault into at least three different prongs, leaving each vulnerable to Confederate counterattack. Griffin knew his division's unprotected right flank would cause problems for him—which it did. Confederates appeared there and punished him. His left-most brigades had better luck, but they, too, eventually ground to a halt and were then driven back.

As Richard Ewell's Confederates filed into place, they immediately began to fortify as they awaited the Federal response to their presence. (fsnmp)

glass," wrote a Federal colonel, "I could plainly see the enemy filing off to the right and left of the road and apparently massing his forces."

The Confederates belonged to Lt. Gen. Richard Ewell's Second Corps. Lee had sent them as the first wave in an attempt to delay the Federal movement while the rest of the Confederate army got into position. As Ewell's men filed from the road into the forest, they began to dig trenches at the crest of a ridge that ran along the western edge of a clearing known as Saunders Field.

"I do not believe that Warren ever had a greater surprise in his life," wrote a staff officer who saw the V Corps commander's reaction when a courier arrived with the news. Lee was supposed to be miles away, yet reports now flooded in indicating an unknown number of Confederates threatened the Federal column.

Warren halted his march immediately. He set up headquarters at Ellwood, which provided him with as good of a view of the tangled Wilderness as he was liable to get, then ordered his men to deploy. He also sent word to Meade who, in turn, forwarded the news to Grant. Grant ordered Warren to pitch into Lee immediately "without giving time for disposition."

To do so, Warren had to shift his men from marching formation into line of battle—and he had to do so in the indomitable thickness of the Wilderness. "Just imagine the difficulty a single unencumbered man would have getting through those thickets," said Harold George of the 139th Pennsylvania, "and then think what a task it was to take a line of battle through those woods; the men encumbered as ours were with knap sacks on backs, three days rations in haversack, gun in hand and 60 rounds of ammunition."

Some of Warren's men began to dig earthworks of their own. At the far right of the line, where the rear guard had been, Warren ordered Griffin to send a force forward to probe the enemy. Griffin balked because his flanks would be unprotected. Sedgwick would eventually

Maj. Gen. Gouverneur K. Warren had temporarily led the II Corps in the fall campaign, but when Winfield Scott Hancock returned to his post, Warren was transferred to command of the V Corps. Many army wags saw him as a possible replacement for Meade should anything happen to the army commander. (loc)

The view of Ayres's brigade as it crossed Saunders Field (top) and the view from the Confederates's perspective as they came out to the woodline to meet Ayres's men (bottom). A swale, visible in the top photo, served to shield the Federals as they got close to the Confederate position (note, in the bottom photo, how the rubber path vanishes at the lip of the swale). (cm)(cm)

arrive to the north of Warren—although not in time to help Griffin—but the Federal position remained highly vulnerable. Struggling against the Wilderness, Warren couldn't deploy his men quickly enough, nor could he get them into one contiguous line.

By 10:30, word arrived that a large Confederate force had appeared on the Orange Plank Road to the south. Lee had apparently sent not one but two spearheads toward the Union column.

Grant managed to stem that crisis by noon, but along the Turnpike, Warren had still not launched an attack. Meade, under pressure from Grant for all-out action, tore into Warren, who in turn tore into Griffin, who continued to demur. When Griffin finally did advance sometime around 12:30, it was against his own better judgment. At least some of his men felt differently, though. "The officers and men all along the line were eager and enthusiastic, and evidently anticipated, without thought of dread, the first fight of the campaign," said one officer.

By one o'clock, Griffin's men reached the eastern edge of Saunders Field. One of the largest open areas in the Wilderness, the unevenly shaped field measured some 400 yards long by 800 yards wide. The Turnpike ran directly down the middle of the field, and a swale bisected it from southeast to northwest. "The last crop of the old field had been corn," said one soldier, "and among its stubble that day were sown the seeds of glory."

On the north side of the turnpike, Federals marched into the clearing, protected somewhat by the ravine as they moved downhill. But as they ascended the far side, Confederates opened fire on them. "Men disappeared as if the earth had swallowed them. . . ." said one of the attacking Federals. "It seemed as if the regiment had been annihilated."

Suddenly, a large body of Confederates appeared on Griffin's unprotected right flank, drawing the rightmost regiments—United States Regulars—out of position to face the new threat. "We were exposed to a terrific cross fire, which mowed down men by scores," one of them recalled. "No troops could stand this and our left broke and ran. This of course made bad worse and the entire line broke."

In spite of the chaos, the 140th New York—a Zouave regiment decked out in bright blue pantaloons, blue shell jackets with bright red piping, and bright red fezzes to match—managed to crest the far ridge. The Confederate brigadier there, General George "Maryland" Steuart, failed to take best advantage of the terrain when he had ordered his men to entrench. His line sat behind the crest of the ridge, rather than in front of it, denying his men the opportunity to fire at Federals crossing the open field. For a few moments, the Federals managed to swarm into the Confederate line before numbers turned against them.

Adding to the chaos, a pair of Union guns wheeled into the middle of Saunders Field and began to fire rounds toward the Confederate works. "[T]here were two terrific explosions in the hollow behind us, accompanied by the crash of shot through the trees, followed by a dense cloud of smoke which completely enveloped us," recalled Porter Farley, a Pennsylvanian still out in the field, trying to advance on the Confederate works. "Taken by surprise by this fire in our rear, we jumped into a gulley which had been worn by the rain beside the road, and in its friendly shelter retreated. . . .The

Two cannon from Battery D of the 1st New York artillery came onto the field to support the Union assault, but their exposed position south of the road in the bottom of the swale—in the middle of the field—left them vulnerable to sniper fire. Once the Federal attack crumpled, Confederates swarmed around the guns. The 1st and 3rd North Carolina captured the pieces, but when a wave of retreating Federals washed across the southern end of the clearing, the 6th Alabama tried to take advantage of the confusion and claim the guns for themselves. Civil War nearly erupted between troops of the two Southern states before the North Carolinians's entire brigade materialized to back up the Tar Heels. (cm)

guns blazed away and we could now see that they were a section of our own artillery planted in the hollow and firing up the road where we had been standing."

The shells exploded into the Confederate line where the New Yorkers were fighting, finally making their

Trapped in the swale in front of the Confederate position, the 140th New York faced the grim prospect of running the gauntlet back across the field to safety. (fsnmp)

position untenable. They collapsed backward into the relative safety of the swale. Casualties among the artillery crews would eventually end the shelling, and the two cannon would fall into Confederate hands. Meanwhile, from the northwest edge of the field, where the Union line had broken, more Confederates swept in behind the New Yorkers, surrounding them. A second Zouave regiment, the 146th New York, also found itself trapped. They soon lost their colonel, David Jenkins. Together, survivors from the two units ran the gauntlet in retreat, "creating a fantastic spectacle as the wearers ran to and fro over the field, firing and shouting."

South of the Turnpike, the Federals fared a little better. The brigade of Brig. Gen. Joseph Bartlett broke through the Confederate line and routed the men of Brig. Gen. John M. "Rum" Jones. Jones, trying to rally his men and vowing to die before giving another inch, was shot dead from his horse. Confusion caused even more Confederates to withdraw. Soon, recalled a Pennsylvania officer, "[o]n we went, o'er briar, o'er brake, o'er logs and o'er bogs through the underbrush and overhanging limbs, for about three quarters of a mile, yelling like so many demons."

"[T]he advance through the woods was not accomplished without serious loss," conceded a member of the 118th Pennsylvania. "Many a brave fellow bit the dust as the charge was made. . . ."

West Point classmates of Brig. Gen. John M. Jones nicknamed him "Rum" Jones because of his fondness for drink. The Confederate brigadier was killed during the May 5 fighting. (loc)

Bartlett's men soon found themselves isolated, and they began to take fire on their flanks. They turned about and made their way back to Saunders Field, first in good order then pell-mell. Many barely avoided being captured, including Bartlett. "His horse was killed, part of his clothing was shot away, but he fortunately escaped with a few bruises," an observer noted.

By 2:30 p.m., the assaults along the Orange Turnpike were over. Meade tried to renew action less than an hour later, sending Sedgwick's corps against

After his brigade collapsed into chaos, Brig. Gen. Joseph Bartlett (right) unexpectedly found himself in a tight spot. A member of the 20th Maine described the scene:

(loc)

"[A] Union officer . . . also came out into the field, not twenty rods from the rebel line. He was on horseback; not a staff officer was with him; his uniform was torn and bloody; blood was trickling from several wounds in his face and head. . . . The rebels saw him, the moment he emerged from the forest, and called upon him to surrender, while a wild yell rang along their line as they saw their fancied prize. But they did not know the man with whom they had to deal. Shaking his fist at them in defiance, he put spurs to his horse and dashed away. He was a target for every rifle in the rebel line. Five hundred guns were pointed at him, and five hundred bullets whistled around him, the enemy pursuing as they fired. It was a brilliant ride for life. . . . Over one-half the distance across that field had been passed, and yet . . . [a] deep ditch must be crossed before they could gain the cover of the forest. . . . The horse and rider evidently saw the obstacle at the same moment and prepared to meet it. . . . For a moment

Barlett popped out of the woods along the south edge of Saunders Field and then made a harrowing dash to safety. (cm)

I thought they were safe, but rebel bullets pierced the horse, and turning a complete somersault he fell stone dead, burying the rider beneath him as he fell. Again the rebels cheered and rushed on, but to my surprise, the officer, with the assistance of a few wounded soldiers, extricated himself from his dead horse, ran across the edge of the field, and made his escape."

the Confederate position, but poor organization and the thick Wilderness itself prevented success. For the rest of the day, most of the significant fighting across the battlefield shifted to the south.

"All nature seems to expect some awful shock," a member of the Stonewall Brigade had said as he'd waited for the day's action to begin.

The fighting in Saunders Field on May 5 proved shocking enough, indeed—but the real shock, the one nobody yet knew, was the fighting between the two armies that had started in this field would continue unabated all summer long.

At Saunders Field (Stop 4A)

The Wilderness Exhibit Shelter was built in the early 1960s for the Civil War Centennial. (cm)

The remains of Wilderness Military Cemetery #1 (below, left) can still be seen today: subtle indentations in the ground to the left of the rubberized path where it enters the treeline (below, right). (fsnmp)(cm)

The Wilderness Exhibit Shelter that stands in Saunders Field is open year round and staffed seasonally. Built during the Civil War Centennial, the shelter houses displays that offer an overview of the battle.

Also on-hand is one of the most familiar interpretive features of the battlefield: a battle painting by the late Sidney King. King, a former resident of nearby Caroline Count, painted dozens of scenes for national parks throughout Virginia. Much of his work is now on display at an art center that bears his name in Bowling Green. (See *Strike Them a Blow: Battle Along the North Anna* for more information on King and his work.) King's work, beloved by generations of visitors, was not without flaw: he incorrectly attributes the field to "Sanders" rather than "Saunders," and he mislabels the Higgerson farm as "Hagerson."

At the time of the battle, Saunders Field was a bit larger than it is now. The eastern treeline on the north side of the road, for instance, sat farther back, as did the field's northern tree line. Hidden in the woods there is a Park Service maintenance building that used to be part of the Civilian Conservation Corps camp that once occupied the field (see appendix). Aside from the maintenance building, the CCC also left its mark on the site

From the exhibit shelter, a rubberized path leads up to the Confederate earthworks just inside the tree line. Along the way, the path passes a monument for the 140th New York Infantry, a unit raised from around Rochester. The 140th entered the fray with 529 men and lost 23 killed, 118 wounded, and 114 missing—a casualty rate of 48 percent.

Just before the tree line, between the path and the road, several light depressions are visible on the ground.

Confederates dug their works behind the crest of the ridge, which offered them protection as they built the works but which proved an awful place to fight from because the ridge offered shielding for the advancing Federals. Confederates had to leave the safety of their works and advance to the treeline to meet the threat, then use the works as a fallback position where they could rally. (cm)

Soldiers killed in battle were buried here in June 1865 in one of two national cemeteries established on the battlefield. While the number of interments is not known, estimates vary from anywhere between 108 and 350, all buried in mass graves. The soldiers were later disinterred and moved to Fredericksburg National Cemetery.

Inside the tree line, the Confederate earthworks snake along the crest of the ridge and often sit behind the actual crest itself. They dug in here because the topography provided protection as they worked, but the position proved to be less than ideal because the topography also shielded Federals as they approached. Confederates had to abandon their works and advance to the treeline to engage the attackers. When the fight deteriorated into hand-to-hand combat, Confederates fell back to their works and rallied there, even as Union artillery began to crash in among them. Federals were eventually forced to withdraw.

From this position, the Gordon Flank Attack hiking trail winds 2.1 miles into the woods. This trail follows the action of May 6, 1864, recounted in Chapter 13. "The trail passes through a maze of earthworks built at various stages of the battle," the Park Service explains. "In several places, Union earthworks captured by Confederates were re-faced and incorporated into the Southern defensive line."

→ **TO Stop 4B**

Route 20 can be extremely busy with fast-moving traffic, so exercise caution as you leave the exhibit shelter parking lot. Turn right and drive 0.1 miles to the crest of the hill. Turn left onto Hill-Ewell Drive and pull over in the parking area on the left.

GPS: N 38.31562, W 77.75915

At Saunders Field (Stop 4B)

The bronze tablet on the U.D.C. monument has an errant apostrophe in "it's" text. (cm)

A map, even one marked with elevation lines, presents only a two-dimensional view of a battlefield. However, the three-dimensional features of the landscape frequently dictate the events and outcomes of battle. Saunders Field provides some useful illustrations because the cleared space gives modern visitors a look at the undulating terrain elsewhere obscured by trees.

The undulations of the ground frequently served to funnel advancing soldiers in odd directions, causing misdirection and delay. When covered with thick undergrowth, as they were throughout the Wilderness, such topographical features made straight and clear navigation nearly impossible.

A swale cuts across Saunders Field, from southeast to northwest. As soldiers marched down into the swale, the uphill slope shielded them from enemy fire. When the 140th New York crossed the field, for instance, the first volley from Confederates went well over their heads. But because of the diagonal cut of the swale, Federals advancing up the slope south of the road found themselves vulnerable to fire from the very same Confederates who couldn't shoot at the advancing New Yorkers.

Likewise, artillerists who set up pieces near the bottom of the swale couldn't see their targets over the crest of the hill. Eventually, they turned their cannons to face northwest, up the length of the swale, where they could see Confederates emerging from the woods on the Union flank.

The bottom of the swale gets marshy during rainy spells. Dozens of other such low-lying areas across the Wilderness created unexpected wet spots that impeded movement—and in the heavy foliage, such wet spots proved almost impossible to detect in advance.

The Orange Turnpike, which brought both armies to the battlefield, still bisects the field today as modern

A historical view of Saunders Field (top) and a modern view (bottom), as seen from the edge of the field by today's Hill-Ewell Drive. "It was narrow, deserted," said V Corps staff officer Morris Schaff, describing Saunders Field, "occupying a depression between two irregular ridges, and extended (on) both sides of the Pike which crossed it a little diagonally nearer its southern end. The east and west sides sloped down to a gully in the middle, the scored-out bed of a once trembling primeval wood-stream; in its palmy days the Pike crossed it on a wooden bridge. The field was known as the Saunders or Palmer field, and was about eight hundred yards wide. It was about the only open, sunshiny spot. . . ." (fsnmp)(cm)

Route 20. In Saunders Field, it's easy to envision how a column of troops marching down the road could file off to one side of the road or the other and, taking advantage of the open space, quickly spread out into line of battle. That also makes it easy to envision why Lee wanted to avoid giving the Federal army any opportunity to do that.

By walking across the field, a visitor will see how dramatically the view changes from spot to spot, how perspectives shift, how the land unfolds. Unseen dips and rises will reveal themselves.

It's all visible in Saunders Field—one of the few places in the Wilderness where anything was visible at all.

Along the Federal Line Trail

The Federal Line Trail runs 3.6 miles one way, starting at the battlefield's picnic area and coming out at Longstreet's wounding site along the Plank Road. Along the way, the trail bisects V Corps earthworks (right center) and parallels other works Federals built on the western edge of the Lacy property to protect the artillery there. On the path's northeast leg,

it passes by a set of these extremely well-preserved artillery emplacements—12 lunettes that once sat in open ground but are now located inside the trees (top). They rise out of the forest on the path's eastern side (on the left if coming from the picnic area). In the photograph, the lunettes are difficult to see, but the shadows spilling across them help define their shape. Elsewhere along the path, hikers can see damage left by Hurricane Isabel, which ravaged parts of the forest in 2003 (above right). (cm)(cm)(cm)

Picnic area trailhead GPS: 38.31172, W 77.75160

Today, the view from the Lacy family cemetery at Ellwood (top) belies the thunder of war that once echoed across this same area on May 5, 1864 (above). The artillery lunettes along the Federal Line Trail are located in the far treeline visible in the top photo. (cm)(loc)

→ **TO STOP 5**

Continue along Hill-Ewell Drive. The Higgerson Farm will be 0.8 miles on the right. On the way, you may choose to stop at the park's picnic area—0.6 miles from Stop 4B on the left—and hike the Federal Line Trail (see below). Otherwise, parking for the Higgerson Farm is 0.2 miles past the picnic area. Park on the right.

GPS: N 38.30862, W 77.74979

The Sprawl of Battle

CHAPTER SIX

MAY 5, 1864

Two roads, roughly parallel, stabbed into the right flank of the Union column as it marched south on May 5. The northern road, the Orange Turnpike, shot straight; the southern, the Orange Plank Road, took a less direct route.

Lieutenant General Richard Ewell's column of Confederates, marching along the northern road, thus reached the Union position sooner than Lt. Gen. A. P. Hill's column, marching along the less-direct southern road.

And so, as more Confederates came to the field along the Plank Road, fighting in the Wilderness—which started along the Turnpike—shifted southward as the day progressed.

When Griffin sent his Federals sweeping across Saunders Field at 1:00 p.m., Brig. Gen. James Wadsworth advanced his men to the south, protecting Griffin's left flank. Whereas Griffin's men moved through one of the largest open spaces in the Wilderness, Wadsworth had the Wilderness itself to push through. His advance quickly stalled.

Colonel Roy Stone and his Bucktails, at the center of Wadsworth's formation, had particular difficulty. His brigade advanced along the southern edge of Wilderness Run, a swampy depression one Pennsylvanian described as the "champion mud hole of mud holes." On either side of Stone's men, the rest of Wadsworth's division moved forward, crossing a clearing known as Spring Hill, the site of the Higgerson Farm. With Stone's men literally bogged down, a large gap developed in Wadsworth's line.

And into that gap poured the Confederates of Brig. Gen. John B. Gordon, freshly arrived on the field from the Orange Turnpike.

The ruins of the Higgerson house sit in tree-shaded heaps. (cm)

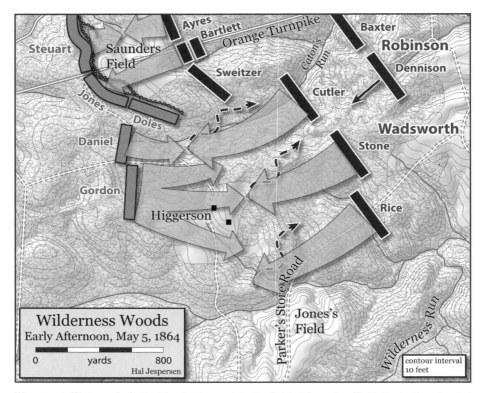

WILDERNESS WOODS—As both sides fed troops into the fight at Saunders Field, the battle extended southward into the dense forest south of the clearing. The foliage foiled Federal attempts to get into a solid line of battle, leaving a gap in the line exploited by Confederates under Brig. Gen. John Brown Gordon.

When things had been going badly for Confederates along the south end of Saunders Field, Gordon had been directed into line to bolster the Confederate position. With the threat from Bartlett contained, Gordon continued to shift farther southward to extend the Confederate line. What he found, though, was an infantry commander's dream: to the north and south of him, he saw the unprotected flanks of lines of Union soldiers.

"Looking down that line from Grant's right toward his left, there first would have been seen a long stretch of blue uniforms, then a short stretch of gray, then another still longer of blue, in one continuous line. . . ." Gordon later wrote with much enthusiasm in his hyperbolic memoir. "In such a crisis, when moments count for hours, when the fate of a command hangs upon instantaneous decision, the responsibility of the commander is almost overwhelming; but the very extremity of the danger electrifies his brain to abnormal activity."

Instead of crossing the field where he would've encountered Stone's men in the bog, Gordon swung

The Bucktails waded into a wilderness that rivaled anything any of them had seen in their native "Pennsylvania wilds." (loc)

some of his men northward and some southward, where they pitched into "the astounded Federals, shattering them. . . ."

Among the first Federals hit were the usually stout veterans of the famed Iron Brigade. "[T]here was a great outburst of musketry," remembered Rufus Dawes of the 6th Wisconsin, which served in the brigade. "There came the enemy stretching as far as I could see through the woods, and rapidly advancing and firing upon us." For the first time in their career, the Iron Brigade broke and ran. "The brush served us well," Dawes admitted. "Our smaller body of men could move faster than the heavy lines of the enemy could follow." Their retreat triggered mass confusion in the Union ranks, halting Wadsworth's assault.

While most of Gordon's men had peeled away for their sudden flank attacks, two of his regiments did drive forward into Stone's mired men, who, like the Iron Brigade, fell back in chaos. Many wound up as prisoners.

Up and down Wadsworth's line, survivors of the failed advance tumbled back toward Ellwood, where they mingled with survivors from Griffin's advance across Saunders Field. Large groups of soldiers, said one Union officer, crowded the area and came "pouring out of the woods in great confusion and almost panic stricken." In the open ground around the Lacy house, they began to construct a log breastwork. Confederates soon appeared and were rebuffed only after a sharp firefight, bolstered on the Federal side by artillery posted on the ridge near the house.

As Gordon's men returned from their advance, 10 or 20 Georgians under Maj. James Van Valkenburg stumbled upon 7th Pennsylvania Reserves, a regiment sent to the Higgerson farm from the south to lend support to the Federal advance. Van Valkenburg tricked the 272 Pennsylvanians into surrendering—a doubly sweet bit of

Brig. Gen. James Wadsworth commanded some of the most storied troops in the V Corps, but they were about to have an ill-starred May, starting on the 5th and 6th. (loc)

trickery because the regiment had captured him a year and a half earlier at the battle of Fredericksburg.

*   *   *

Pennsylvanian Samuel Crawford, a former surgeon, had impressive facial hair even by the standards of the well-whiskered Army of the Potomac. (loc)

The Pennsylvanians had been sent from the nearby Chewning farm, where Federals under Brig. Gen. Samuel Crawford had been posted. They had marched at the head of the Federal column that morning and, when Ewell's arrival near Saunders Fields necessitated a halt, they took up position "on high ground, so that we could plainly see the store and the Orange Plank Road which runs by it," one artillerist later reported.

At 8:00 a.m., Crawford's men had first spotted what appeared to be Confederate cavalry sparring with a detachment of Federal cavalry about a mile to the southwest at Parker's Store. Crawford sent a regiment equipped with rapid-fire Spencer repeating rifles to help the Federal horsemen.

By 10:00, though, Crawford realized the Confederate cavalry actually rode at the head of a large infantry force. He sent word back to Meade who, soon after, withdrew the advanced regiment. The Federal cavalry withdrew, as well. The Confederates advanced eastward on the Plank Road unopposed. Crawford held his position as they passed to his south, moving eastward toward the intersection with Brock Road.

When Crawford heard fighting erupt to his north—Wadsworth's general advance—he sent half of his division to help. Shortly thereafter, he suddenly recognized the vulnerability of his own lonely position atop the Chewning high ground. Confederates could approach him not only from the south but, because they had advanced so far along the Orange Plank Road, they could approach from the east, as well. And with Wadsworth in retreat, Crawford had no support.

Sometime around 2:30 p.m., under orders from Warren, the rest of Crawford's men withdrew.

→ **TO STOP 6**

Continue along Hill-Ewell Drive for 1 mile. Park on the right.

GPS: N 38.29640, W 77.74451

At the Higgerson Farm

A short walking trail leads to a pile of rubble that had once been the home of Permelia Higgerson. A soldier described the property as "a small hut and tobacco barn built of logs" situated in "a small field." Although the house survived the battle, it burned down in the 1930s. The chimneys survived but later collapsed in on themselves.

Permelia Higgerson's hardscrabble home looked as rough as the wilderness that surrounded it. (fsnmp)

Permelia was home at the time of the battle. She taunted Federal soldiers as they swept across her property, predicting they'd be turned back. They were.

The fighting that swirled around her property consisted of men commanded by Confederates John Brown Gordon and Junius Daniel and Federal James Wadsworth. Of the three, only Gordon would survive the Overland Campaign (and the war). Wadsworth would be killed the next day along the Orange Plank Road; Daniel would die a week later at Spotsylvania.

The Higgerson farm sat in a clearing atop a steep knoll, still kept clear today. (cm)

Homeplaces in the Swirl of War

CHAPTER SEVEN

MAY 5-7, 1864

The Chewning Farm sat atop a long, open plateau that rose like an island out of the forest. From the high ground, visitors could see Virginia's Blue Ridge far to the west. Closer, just a few miles to the northeast of the two-and-a-half story farmhouse, visitors could see the Wilderness Tavern. For entertainment, family members living in the farmhouse would sometimes use field glasses to watch pigeons strut about on the tavern roof.

To the southwest, visitors could plainly see Parker's Store a mile away. A sun-dappled country lane ran down to the abandoned store from the hilltop.

The farm, christened "Mount View" by its owners, William and Permelia Chewning, had sprung up on the plateau sometime before 1836. Compared to their neighbors at the Ellwood plantation, the Chewnings owned a small farm: some 150 acres, including the 80 acres of cleared land along the top of the plateau, where they grew wheat, rye, oats, corn, and tobacco. Thirteen slaves worked the land and lived in cabins that sat to the east of the farm's big barn.

The Chewnings had 10 children, spaced so far apart that the eldest had married and moved away before the youngest were even born. By 1860, on the eve of the war, only the youngest two remained at home, 34-year-old Jane and 26-year-old Absalom. William and Absalom worked the farm side by side. Father also taught son the family tradition of shoemaking.

One of the family's other daughters lived less than a mile away. Also named Permelia, she had married Benjamin Higgerson, a farmer, and together they raised four children. They had a tobacco barn near the house as well as a family cemetery.

Ellwood went from being summer home to V Corps headquarters. (cm)

The Chewnings and Higgersons mostly avoided the war, and the war avoided them. Only Absalom served any time in the Confederate army—a seven-day stint cut short for health reasons. After that, the government assigned him a job at Catharine Furnace, as a blacksmith, where they called him "Boss Smith."

When the war did arrive, though, it first did so in quiet, tragic fashion. In the late fall of 1862, Permelia Higgerson took into her home a wounded Confederate. Too late, the family discovered he had smallpox. Benjamin contracted the disease and, on Christmas Day, he died. Permelia buried him in the family cemetery near the house.

Permelia Higgerson and her son, Edgar (fsnmp)

William Chewning died the following June as the result of an accident at a local gristmill. By that point, most of the Chewning's slaves had deserted the family. Only Thomas, a 50-year-old slave who served as Absalom's personal attendant, remained.

Federal soldiers moved through the area in the fall of 1863 and again in the spring of 1864. Like many of her neighbors, Permelia Chewning placed her silverware in boxes and buried them in her garden for safekeeping. When Northern soldiers finally did pay her a visit in early May, Permelia was home alone. By afternoon, the soldiers—elements of General Samuel Crawford's brigade—had butchered the pigs from the farm's hog pen and, after bullying Permelia out of her home, set to roasting pork in the big kitchen fireplace. One of Permelia's cousins, riding in on horseback that evening, tricked the Federals into surrendering even as Permelia made her way through the darkening Wilderness to the safety of a neighbor's house. It was well she fled, for early the next morning sharp fighting broke out in the fields around her hilltop house.

May 5 turned out to be far more eventful for Permelia's daughter down at the Higgerson farm. Federal troops swept across her property in the early afternoon, much to her chagrin. A Pennsylvanian heard the younger Permelia express "her views on the matter in strong language," calling the Federals "a pack of cowardly Yankees." After Confederates repulsed the Union advance, the jubilant woman taunted and derided the Federals as they retreated.

Other local families had encounters of their own

with Federal soldiers. A detachment of New Yorkers, trying to find the rest of their regiment, sought out the "lord of the manor" at an unidentified farmhouse, probably belonging to the Webb family, to serve as a guide. "Couldn't think of it," the farmer replied. "When I'm gone, who knows who might tote off my wife and young uns. Couldn't think of it, sir." "No excuses will do, sir," the Federal captain replied. The farmer's daughter then intervened. "Oh, sir!" she said, "you would not think of taking my father? What should we do were some accident to befall him?" The captain promised no harm would come to the father, so the daughter asked to go along, too.

Another young girl, 4-year-old Eliza Tapp, lived with her widowed mother and grandmother in a cabin to the southeast of Mount View near the Orange Plank Road. The mother, Catherine Tapp, rented the 40-acre farmstead from J. Horace Lacy, the owner of Ellwood. Plum and cherry trees surrounded the Tapp home, which also had a corncrib, a stable, and another outbuilding. Eliza heard the sounds of cannon and mistook it for thunder. A great storm was brewing, she thought. Not long after, she and her family fled westward down the Orange Plank Road, and she remembered the patter of large raindrops on the road around her. Only later did she learn that the raindrops were Minié balls.

Any farmer's field, any open space around a family farmhouse, attracted the armies as they grappled against each other in the bramble-choked forest. Fighting swirled into those open spaces, displacing the people who lived there or forcing them into hiding.

The Chewnings's farm attracted particular attention because of the view it offered of the surrounding countryside. In the late afternoon of May 7, Robert E. Lee met with his subordinate A. P. Hill on the front porch

Ohio artist George L. Frankenstein captured Catherine Tapp's modest log home in watercolor circa 1866—one of five local war-related landmarks he painted in the Fredericksburg area. (fsnmp)

In the 1930s, former Park Service Historian Ralph Happel sat down with Eliza "Phenie" Tapp, who still lived on her family homestead, to collect her reminiscences of the battle. (fsnmp)

of the house, and there they observed that the Union army was in motion.

Later that week, when Absalom returned to the house from the furnace, traveling along a narrow path through the dark woods, he stumbled over bodies strewn across the pathway. His house, he discovered, was deserted. He eventually found his mother, and with his former slave, Thorton, the three returned to Mount View.

"They did have a home to come back to, even if it was in an awful mess," recalled Absalom's granddaughter, many years later, passing along family lore; "the floors in the big front room were very blood stained, and blood would not wash out of the wooden floor boards, so they had to be taken up and replaced. The fences were torn down as well as some of the smaller servants cabins. Yes the house was still there—as well as the barn and Absalom's workshop, but they were all riddled with bullets and everything inside was a terrible mess, all broken and torn." Even the silverware buried in the vegetable garden was missing.

Like so many of their neighbors, the Chewnings returned after the battle and did the only thing they could: They tried to rebuild their lives in the hardscrabble Wilderness.

At the Chewning Farm

The Chewning farm sat atop a high plateau that first belonged to the Federals and then fell into Confederate hands. Federals then tried to retake it, to no avail. In the process, they nearly took Third Corps commander Lt. Gen. A. P. Hill, who was standing with his staff near the house when Federals pushed into the clearing. Hill calmly told his men, "Mount, walk your horses, and don't look back." It was Hill's second such near-miss in two days. Reinforcements from his corps soon arrived and drove the Federals away. "I wanted to fire on you," one of the Federal prisoners grumbled later to one of Hill's staff members, "but my colonel said you were farmers riding from the house."

That afternoon, Ambrose Burnside was ordered to retake the hill but failed. Instead, Hill and Lee used the location for reconnaissance. Staff members cut a hole in the roof, from which Lee could see the hub of the Union army around Ellwood.

Built circa 1836, the house sustained heavy damage during the battle, but it survived until 1947, when it was destroyed by fire.

A quarter-mile walking path (top) leads to the plateau where the Chewning farm (above) once stood. (cm)(fsnmp)

Ellwood in the Swirl

By the evening of May 5, small groups of orderlies, clerks, teamsters, and cooks milled about on the grounds around Ellwood. They sat, in groups of twos and threes, around campfires. Some, using their jackets as pillows, had lain down to sleep despite the clatter of cooking pots and the braying of donkeys and horses from the nearby wagons. Nearby, a line of artillery stood silent—a sharp contrast to the thunder they had bellowed all day.

Inside, in the large, high-ceilinged parlor to the left of the front door, lit by the flickering light of several candles and a globe lantern, Maj. Gen. Gouverneur K. Warren sat at a table and looked at numbers. "[H]is long, coal-black hair was streaming away from his finely expressive forehead, the only feature rising unclouded above the habitual gloom of his duskily sallow face," remembered one of his staff officers.

In a room in Ellwood made to resemble General Warren's headquarters there, the bric-a-brac of war intermingle with household items on a fireplace mantel. (cm)

Warren had chosen Ellwood as his headquarters that morning. The open hills around the house provided a perfect platform for artillery—especially important because of a lack of good artillery positions closer to the front. Ellwood also offered Warren easy routes of communication to portions of his corps down both the Orange Turnpike and Parker's Store Road.

At 2:30 that afternoon, Grant and Meade paid Warren a visit. Even from the high, clear ground of Ellwood, which afforded a good view, it took the generals nearly half an hour to get oriented to the battleground because the Wilderness presented such a confusing landscape.

By then, those wounded from the battle along the Turnpike had begun streaming back from the front. Surgeons had erected field hospitals near the northern border of the Lacy property, around the Wilderness Tavern, and they set about their own bloody work.

Warren, while sitting in this room at a desk much like this one, compiled casualty reports—which he urged his staff to falsify. "It will never do . . . to make a showing of such heavy losses," he told them. (cm)

It was with his chief surgeon and his chief of staff that Warren met now as they pored over the numbers of killed and wounded during the first day of battle. "It will never do, to make a showing of such heavy losses," Warren finally said. The numbers, he suggested, would have to be softened.

The Army of the Potomac departed from the

Wilderness with the true scope of horror downplayed, yet the dead and wounded left an everlasting mark on Ellwood. The 26 graves dug within a few hundred yards of the house hardly even began to tell the full story. "Many graves were ploughed over by the tenant, before I returned to the County," wrote J. Horace Lacy in 1866. "Therefore other graves [are] unmarked which I could not designate, though the places are known."

After the battle of Chancellorsville, when the house had been used as a hospital, blood had stained its hardwood floors. After the battle of the Wilderness, blood had drenched Ellwood's very soil.

⟶ TO STOPS 7 AND 8

Carefully merge back onto Hill-Ewell Drive and follow the road 1.2 miles. You will come to a pull-off for Tapp Field, Stop 7, on the right (see next page).

GPS: N 38.29332, W 77.72712

To reach Stop 8, merge back on to Hill-Ewell Drive and travel 0.2 miles to the intersection with Brock Road. Turn left. Follow Brock Road one mile. The parking area for the Brock Road/Plank Road intersection (Stop 8) will be on the right.

GPS: N 38.30087, W 77.70938

The Wilderness today has far more homes than it did in 1864. Three large gated communities are located on ground where battle once raged: Lake of the Woods on the north edge of the battlefield, Fawn Lake on the southeast edge, and Lake Wilderness, visible (above) along the southern half of Hill-Ewell Drive. (cm)

At Widow Tapp Field (Stop 7–North Edge)

The walking path from the north edge of Tapp Field (above) connects with a loop that begins at the southwest corner. (cm)

The eastern edge of Tapp Field offers a good point of orientation for the see-saw battle that swung back and forth on this sector of the battlefield on May 5 and 6.

A line of works parallels Hill-Ewell Drive in this area on the eastern side of the road (see photo previous page). Confederates threw up these works on the evening of May 6 after most of the heaviest fighting here had already occurred. A. P. Hill, believing his men would be relieved overnight May 5-6, told his men not to fortify their position and were thus caught off guard by the Federal assault on morning of May 6; Confederates did not make that same mistake again.

On the morning of May 6, Federals advanced from the east (the side of the road where the earthworks are). However, on the afternoon of May 5, some Federal skirmishers appeared here from the north. A short walk out into the field here offers a view of the area from which they appeared—a spillover from the fight boiling between the Higgerson and Chewning farms. The Federals found quite a surprise when they finally reached this clearing: a small cluster of Confederate officers. It was Lee, Hill, and Jeb Stuart, consulting over the morning's events. Stuart stared defiantly at the approaching Federals; Lee calmly walked to his horse, mounted, and trotted away; Hill jumped to his feet and ran to safety. The Federals seemed just as startled; although within pistol range, they turned around and faded back into the woods.

The Confederate officers had been relaxing near the Widow Tapp house. From this perspective, the house would have stood at the far-middle edge of the field near the right tree line; a walking trail from Stop 9 provides access to the site today.

Fawn Lake, a gated community on the southeast edge of the battlefield, consists of roughly 2,300 acres. The community has worked with the National Park Service on several occasions to protect battlefield resources, including earthworks and portions of the abandoned railroad cut. (cm)

Crisis Along the Plank Road

CHAPTER EIGHT
MAY 5, 1864

The Confederate advance along Orange Plank Road not only brought the Third Corps to the battle later than Ewell's men to the north because the road ran with more twists and turns, but it intersected the Federal position farther to the east than the north road did. That meant A.P. Hill's corps on the south road had farther to march to reach the Federals. Skirmishes with the 5th New York Cavalry and the 13th Pennsylvania Reserves slowed him further.

But when Hill finally arrived, he nearly placed the Federal army in an untenable position—as Crawford discovered first-hand when he found himself suddenly isolated at the Chewning farm. On a larger scale, though, Hill's advance threatened to cut the entire Federal army in two. The Plank Road intersected another key road, the Brock Road, and if Hill captured that intersection, he would off Winfield Scott Hancock's II Corps, which was marching hard down the Brock Road to join the rest of the Union army. If Hancock didn't hurry, he'd find Confederates waiting for him instead.

This was the crisis Grant had learned of midmorning, even as he waited for events to unfold in Saunders Field. Meade reacted to the news—sent to him by Crawford—by directing the lead elements of John Sedgwick's VI Corps to hurry to the crucial intersection. Brigadier General George Getty and his staff, riding at the vanguard of the column, arrived there at 12:30 p.m. "Surrounded by his staff and orderlies, with his headquarters flag flying overhead, he took post directly at the intersection," recounted Getty's chief of staff, Hazard Stevens.

Getty's party arrived not a moment too soon. A

The Alexander Hays memorial sits on 0.6-acres of land a little east of the actual spot of Hays's mortal wounding, which was deep in the woods. A marker there would not have been visible to passing travellers. (cm)

Brig. Gen. George Getty's shrewd theatrics proved just the trick to stall Confederates until Federal reinforcements could secure the Brock Road/Plank Road intersection. (loc)

Had Maj. Gen. Henry Heth approached the Federal position with more vigor, the battle would have unfolded differently. However, the previous July, as the army's vanguard headed into Gettysburg, Heth had been scolded for being too aggressive. In the Wilderness, he applied the lesson Lee taught him—at exactly the most inopportune time for the Army of Northern Virginia, it seems. (loc)

cluster of Federal horsemen burst past "like a flock of wild geese" and were soon out of sight, "a few barely pausing to cry out that the infantry were coming down the road in force. . . ." Sure enough, Getty could see the Confederates advancing toward him down the Orange Plank Road—in ones and twos, at first, but then as in increasingly inexorable tide.

"We must hold this point at any risk," Getty told his staff. "Our men will be up soon." To buy time, he began barking out orders and making a show of his position, hoping to bluff any Confederates who might see him into thinking he was directing a large body of men and not just his own headquarters staff.

"[A] bullet went whistling overhead," Stevens recalled, "and another and another, and then the leaden hail came faster and faster over and about the little group until its destruction seemed imminent and inevitable."

Getty's infantry arrived "running like greyhounds," filing into the intersection around him. "The distance was nearly two miles, and part of the road was narrow and muddy, but the command pressed rapidly forward and reached the crossing just in time," wrote one of Getty's Vermonters. "We were not a minute too soon." The lead brigade, Frank Wheaton's, quickly formed into ranks and opened fire, stymieing the Confederate advance.

The bulk of the Confederates had come within a few hundred yards of the intersection, but some skirmishers reached as close as 30 yards. Robert E. Lee will "whop you sure," one of them boasted when taken prisoner. "Sure enough, Robert E. hasn't many men, but what he's got are right good ones, and I reckon you'll find it out before you leave here."

The Federals had won the race, but they needed to hold on until Hancock's II Corps could arrive.

* * *

Getty's quick move and clever theatrics stemmed the first crisis, although that also had much to do with Getty's Confederate counterpart, Maj. Gen. Henry Heth.

Lee had given Heth discretionary orders to "occupy the Brock Road if you could do so without bringing on a general engagement." Heth had been under similar orders the previous July, on an excursion into the town of Gettysburg, Pennsylvania, where he had allowed himself to get drawn into a fight that evolved into the most famous battle in the history of the continent. Unsure about the size of the Federal force he now faced at the Brock Road intersection, and whether contact would trigger a general engagement, Heth opted not to make an issue of it.

Getty would have been willing to leave well enough

alone, too, perhaps, but orders arrived from Meade for him to attack. Hancock's II Corps—the portion of the army that would have been cut off had Confederates captured the intersection—began filing in behind Getty. They had marched that morning south from Chancellorsville toward Todd's Tavern but, as the situation at the Wilderness began to boil, Meade ordered Hancock to march north and reinforce Getty at the intersection.

With the extra weight now behind him, Getty pushed forward. "The lines struggled and pushed their way through the dense thickets, becoming more and more crooked and disordered, and soon drew the fire of the enemy. . ." wrote Hazard Stevens. "[T]he contest at once became a heavy pounding match between masses of brave and determined men."

Getty didn't know it, but Heth outnumbered him, so when they advanced, Getty's men quickly got the worst of it. It was, said a North Carolinian, "a butchery pure and simple."

One of the first of Hancock's units into the fray, the brigade of Brig. Gen. Alexander Hays, suffered severely, taking 1,390 casualties, the most of any Federal brigade during the battle. Among the killed—Hays himself, shot from his horse by a bullet to the head.

"The woods would light up with the flashes of musketry as if with lightning," wrote a New Yorker in Hays's brigade, "while the incessant roar of the volleys sound like the crashing of thunderbolts."

"The establishment of a monument to the 12th New Jersey Volunteers is a story of hope, misunderstanding, and ultimately disappointment," says historian Don Pfanz. **"The 12th New Jersey was among the regiments that, with cold steel, retook the burning Federal earthworks from Confederates."** A monument to their work, envisioned by a hometown admirer some 60 years later, was installed but never dedicated because of WWII gas shortages. A second, smaller memorial was added for the Civil War centennial. (cm)

At the Brock Road/Plank Road Intersection

Much of the area around the Brock Road/Plank Road intersection was opened up for interpretation thanks to a $200,000 Federal grant made possible by former U.S. Senator Jim Jeffords of Vermont, who wanted to ensure the role of the Vermonters in the battle was properly highlighted. The grant was used to develop the 0.4-mile walking trail through the area along with the interpretive markers, parking area, and other site improvements. The Vermont Brigade suffered 1,269 casualties during the battle—most of them during the

"Our attack not only held the enemy in check, but put him upon the defensive . . ." said Brig. Gen. Lewis Grant of his Vermonters. "Had it been otherwise . . . the enemy would have secured the [intersection] and completely cut off that corps from the rest of the army." (cm)

fighting on May 5 that ensured Federal control of the vital intersection.

The monument to the Vermont Brigade is one of the newest on the field. Dedicated in 2006, the monument cost $40,000 to construct and $6,000 to install—all paid for by the state of Vermont. The monument weighs 39,000 pounds and rises some seven feet off the ground. The top of the monument was sculpted to resemble Vermont's Camel Hump mountain.

Closer to the intersection itself sit a pair of monuments devoted to the 12th New Jersey. The II Corps unit recaptured logworks in this area on May 6 after the late-afternoon attack by the Confederate First Corps. The larger stone was erected for Memorial Day, 1942, but because of WWII gas rationing, the dedication ceremony was postponed—and then never rescheduled. The monument was rededicated in May of 1964 for the Centennial with the addition of a second, smaller stone.

Three sets of earthworks are visible in this area— one near the New Jersey monuments, one parallel to the near (west) side of Brock Road, and a third in the woods on the far side of the road. The II Corps needed all three lines of works to hold the position against the Confederate attacks of May 6. The set of works that parallels the road stretches well over a mile to the south and are visible even along part of Jackson Trail West.

Historian Gordon Rhea says Brig. Gen. Lewis Grant "adequately compensated for his scant military training with unabashed bravery." (fsnmp)

About 200 yards south of the intersection on the west side of Brock Road, usually buried under leaves and forest debris, sits one of the park's few remaining "N-Markers." In the 1940s, the National Park Service installed as many as 60 stone markers across the park to identify the locations of various units. Most have since been removed or lost, but one remains in the Wilderness to mark the location of the Second Corps's line on May 6th.

About 400 yards to the north of the intersection stands the upturned tube of a 32-pounder howitzer that serves as a memorial to Brig. Gen. Alexander Hays.

"This morning was beautiful," Hays wrote on May 4, 1864, in a letter to his wife. "It might have been an appropriate harbinger of the day of the regeneration of mankind, but it only brought to remembrance, through the throats of many bugles, the duty enjoined upon each one, perhaps before the setting sun, to lay down a life for his country."

It would be the last letter Hays would write to her. The next afternoon, on May 5, Hays would die in the battle that swirled around the Brock Road/ Plank Road intersection.

Rarest of the rare—one of the park's few remaining "N"-markers, hiding in the leaves of the Wilderness. (cm)

But Hays's death would later serve as a symbol of the "regeneration" he'd hoped for. In June 1905, surviving members of 63rd Pennsylvania Infantry, Hays's original unit, dedicated a monument to their fallen general in the vicinity where he was killed.

Former Federals and Confederates alike joined together to dedicate the memorial to Alexander Hays. (fsnmp)

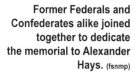

With hat akimbo at a jaunty angle, this sketch of Alexander "Fighting Elleck" Hays captures his likeability. (fsnmp)

At the dedication ceremony Reverend John H. Light "beseeched divine blessing for the movement to heal the wounds of war." Speaker John T. Goolrick, a local judge and Confederate veteran, condemned Southerners who, even then, 41 years after the war, tried to keep sectional tensions alive. Goolrick promised that the Confederate people—especially veterans and their sons—would protect the Hays monument and, every Memorial Day, would decorate it. W.S. Embrey, who'd served in the Confederate army as a major, owned the land where the monument had been raised, and he presented the title for the parcel to the Pennsylvanians. For their part, the Pennsylvanians also made an effort toward reconciliation. On their way to the dedication ceremony, they stopped at the Chancellorsville battlefield to pay their respects to Confederate General "Stonewall" Jackson, who'd fallen there in May 1863. Following the dedication of the Hays Memorial, the veterans also contributed nearly $1,000 toward the Confederate cemetery fund.

In 1959, the National Park Service took possession of the 0.6-acre parcel where the Hays Memorial stands. The site of Hays's death, however, took place in the woods a bit to the west.

"I am not surprised that he met his death at the head of his troops; it was just like him," said Hays's friend, Ulysses Grant. "He was a man who would never follow, but would always lead in battle."

In death, Hays's memory also served to set the good example.

A walking trail at the Brock Road/Plank Road intersection gives visitors the chance to plunge into the Wilderness, although it's far less choked by underbrush now than it was in 1864. (cm)

A Heavy Pounding Match

CHAPTER NINE

MAY 5, 1864—AFTERNOON/EVENING

Back at the Lacy farm, Union commanders could hear the battle building toward a crescendo that would take all afternoon to peak. What began with shots across Saunders Field earlier in the day, then shifted into the woods around Higgerson farm, had shifted southward yet again into a bitter struggle for the Plank Road/Brock Road intersection.

Throughout the day, Grant looked at both fronts in the hope of launching coordinated attacks that would strain Confederate resources. However, the sprawling nature of the battle across a landscape that severely inhibited movement and communication prevented any such coordination—just as Lee had expected. Lee's decision to attack along both roads, creating that sprawl, initially caught Grant off guard and then forced him to spread his army.

As Grant began to adapt, though, his army pummeled Lee's men throughout the afternoon and evening—even as the Confederates successfully kept the Federals pinned in place. "Brave men were falling like autumn leaves," one Union soldier said, "and death was holding high carnival in our ranks."

At the Brock Road/Plank Road intersection, more II Corps soldiers poured into the fight, but the Wilderness continued to blunt their numerical advantage. "When we reached the junction of the roads, we saw the most awful confusion reigning," observed one Mainer. "Numerical superiority was seen here at its worst. There were more troops than could be utilized, almost a huddle. The roads are narrow and the woods and underbrush very dense. It was a dreadfully mixed-up mess."

Lee countered the Federal build-up by shifting more

After it passes beneath Hill-Ewell Drive and escapes from confinement in Lake Wilderness, Wilderness Run winds its way northward to empty into the Rapidan River. (cm)

of Hill's corps into the fight. One of his divisions, that of Maj. Gen. Cadmus Wilcox, had been assigned to stretch north from the Orange Plank Road to hook up with Ewell's line. Lee rerouted Wilcox's men, though, to reinforce Heth.

"The wounded stream out, and fresh troops pour in. Stretchers pass with ghastly burdens, and go back reeking with blood for more," reported correspondent Charles Page of *The New York Tribune*. "Word is brought that the ammunition is failing. 60 rounds fired in one steady, stand-up fight, and that fight is not fought out. Boxes of cartridges are placed on the returning stretchers, and the struggle shall not cease for want of ball and powder."

And so it did not, a Massachusetts soldier said: "For a long time the two lines at close quarters poured deadly volleys into each other without wavering on either side."

By 7:30 p.m., Confederates faced disaster of their own when a Federal unit nearly flanked them; the timely action of a brigade of North Carolinians stopped the Federal movement. Some of the Tar Heels took cover behind "a line of dead Federals so thick as to form a partial breastwork."

"It was novel experience," an officer later recounted, "and seems ghastly enough in the retrospect."

*   *   *

Lee had committed all the men he had available to the battle along the Orange Plank Road. So, when the

division of Union Brig. Gen. James Wadsworth appeared from the northwest—after it had reorganized following its retreat from the field earlier in the afternoon—Lee must have felt his heart sink. Wadsworth's men moved through the very gap in the Confederate line Lee had created when he reassigned Wilcox's men. The Federals angled directly toward the unprotected flank of the Confederate position.

And Lee had no one he could send to stop them.

Wadsworth's men, who had been poorly handled earlier in the day at the Higgerson farm, "came forward, with courageous promptitude . . . seeming anxious to recover what had been lost earlier in the afternoon."

Lee quickly assembled some 150 Alabamians who'd been assigned to guard Federal prisoners in the rear. The Alabamians "went in with a cheer," a soldier wrote—hitting the unsuspecting federals in the flank— "and whatever was before them was driven back." A single battalion had stopped Wadsworth's entire disheartened division.

*   *   *

The fighting along the Orange Plank Road had been "a mere slugging match in a dense thicket of small growth," said one Confederate, "where men but a few yards apart fired through the brushwood for hours, ceasing only when exhaustion and night commanded a rest."

Both exhaustion and night seemed to set in simultaneously. By 9:00 p.m., both armies hunkered down.

"We lay upon the ground surrounded by dead and dying rebel soldiers," wrote Rufus Dawes of the 6th Wisconsin. "The sufferings of these poor men, and their

moans and cries were harrowing. We gave them water from our canteens and all aid that was within our power."

Another soldier thought "the terrible groans of the wounded" mixed with "the mournful sound of the owl and the awful shrill shrieks of the whippoorwill. . . . These birds seemed to mock at our grief and laugh at the groans of the dying."

It was, lamented one Pennsylvanian, "a woeful night . . .":

Throughout the night, as the forest fires, which had blazed since the early afternoon, drew nearer to the poor unfortunates who lay between the lines, their shrieks, cries, and groans, loud and piercing, penetrating, rent the air, until death relieved the sufferer, or the rattle of musketry, that followed the advent of the breaking morn, drowned all the other sounds in its dominating roar.

From the woods north of Saunders Field to the forest around the Brock Road/Plank Road intersection, men of both sides threw up piecemeal lines of haphazard earthworks to protect themselves. "Ours consisted of logs and dirt dug up with bayonets and cast up with tin plates and our need hands," said a member of the 31st Georgia. "Those of the enemy contained also the dead bodies of their own men, besides army blankets, knapsacks, and anything they could find in the darkness of the night."

Heth suggested to Hill they make a concerted effort to straighten and strengthen their part of the line, which wound through the deep forest "like a worm fence, at every angle." Hill demurred, expecting Longstreet's First Corps to arrive at any moment. "I don't propose that your division shall do any fighting tomorrow," Hill told his anxious subordinate. He ordered Heth to rest his men, who had marched and fought all day long. Heth asked Hill to reconsider. "Damn it, Heth, I don't want to hear any more about it," Hill barked. "The men shall not be disturbed."

But Longstreet would not arrive until morning. The Old Warhorse, who had much ground to cover, had not realized how urgently Lee needed his men on the field.

Now aware of the need for haste, Longstreet pushed them. Until he arrived, Lee had no one else to call on; every man then available to Ewell and Hill had been committed.

And so Lee eyed the Orange Plank Road nervously, waiting for Longstreet's arrival from the west and fearing Grant's arrival from beyond Hill's line to the east.

Grant would arrive first.

→ TO STOP 9

Traveling along the Brock Road provides an opportunity to follow the seesaw of battle on May 6.

When you exit the parking area, use extreme caution; Plank Road can be extremely busy. Turn left and travel 1.5 miles. The parking area for Tapp Field will be on the right. Pull in and park. Remain there for the next two chapters.

As you drive toward Stop 9, you will pass the monument for Union Brig. Gen. James Wadsworth on the right, 0.9 miles from the Brock Road/Plank Road intersection. Wadsworth's story will be covered in Chapter 12, but this is the safest opportunity to visit the monument, which will be on the same side of the road you're currently on. Exercise caution when pulling over and pulling back into traffic.

0.2 miles from the Wadsworth monument, on the opposite side of the road, is a monument to Confed. Col. James Nance, killed during Longstreet's counterattack (covered in Chapter 10). There is no safe place to pull over to visit the monument.

GPS: N 38.28928, W 77.72609

Col. James Nance of the 3rd South Carolina Infantry was killed while leading part of Longstreet's newly arrived reinforcements into battle. "We must fight them here," Nance exclaimed, taking his place next to the colors. "Never think of leaving this place!" In fact, Nance never would leave it: moments later, he took a bullet to the head. In August 1912, two veterans from the regiment returned to the battlefield to dedicate a memorial on the spot where their commander vowed to stay. (cm)

The Most Critical Moment

CHAPTER TEN

MAY 6, 1864—MORNING

That Grant sat and whittled away the battle of the Wilderness had less to do with his cool nerves than with his desire to let George Gordon Meade run the Army of the Potomac as Meade saw fit. It was, after all, Meade's army. Grant, as commander of all armies, could have chosen to execute his duties in an office in Washington. That he made his office in the field, with the Union's largest and most visible army, obviously led to some confusion about who was really in charge, so he made an effort to defer to Meade's judgment on all things tactical.

But as the battle wore on, and Grant finally saw the Army of the Potomac in action firsthand, he began to understand why it had such a long legacy of underachieving. The army moved slowly. Communication was inconsistent. Corps commanders exercised wills of their own—wills that frequently demonstrated obstinacy instead of prudent caution. No one dared act with boldness.

This was a problem Meade himself had recognized. Just weeks after the battle of Gettysburg, in July 1863, Meade wrote to his wife: "Another great trouble with me is the want of active and energetic subordinate officers, men upon whom I can depend and rely upon taking care of themselves and commands."

As institutionalized as the army's problems had become, and as much as they hinged on personalities, they still all began at the top, with competent but cautious Meade, who just couldn't seem to get his army to act.

Grant learned that lesson for himself at the Wilderness. As the battle, and later the campaign, unfolded, he began taking a more direct hand in the tactical operation and maneuver of the army. Throughout

Most visitors don't realize that a three-foot chunk of white field quartz at the "Lee to the Rear" site is also a marker, placed there by local residents in 1891 to mark the former burial site of men from John Gregg's famed Texas Brigade. (cm)

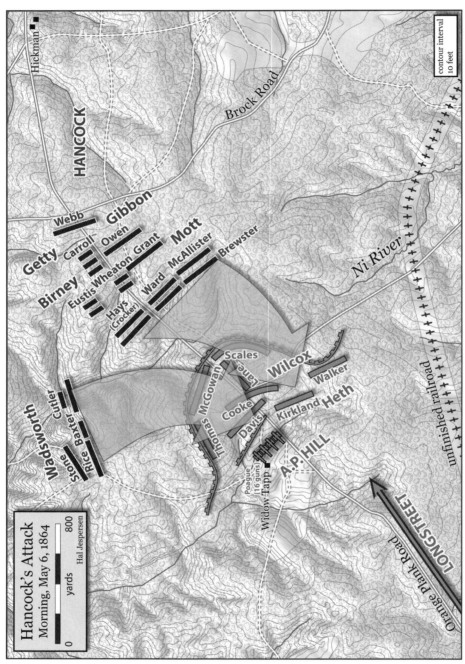

HANCOCK'S ATTACK—Hill's weak defenses gave way easily under Hancock's massive hammer blow. Wadsworth's division, poorly handled twice the day before, vindicated themselves by sweeping in as Hancock's support. Along with Getty's men, that meant parts of three corps participated; Burnside, expected to also lend the weight of the IX Corps, was a no-show. Hill's men, routed, collapsed rearward even as Longstreet finally approached from the west.

May 5, he had encouraged Meade to launch coordinated attacks against the Confederates, felt encouraged by the day's action along the Orange Plank Road. The army had averted a potential crisis there early in the day and, by continually exerting pressure, had nearly precipitated a crisis for the Confederates. He decided to focus his army's energy there the next morning.

Grant gathered with Meade and the Army of the Potomac's three corps commanders to work out the plan. IX Corps commander Maj. Gen. Ambrose Burnside joined them as well. Grant planned a 4:30 assault all along the line, with Burnside's Corps playing a major supporting role on Hancock's front. "He won't be up—I know him well," one of Meade's staff officers later worried. The other corps commanders agreed, so they requested a slightly later start time to accommodate. Grant agreed to a 30-minute postponement.

The delay, it turned out, provided just enough time for Confederates to take the initiative along the Turnpike instead of the Federals. At 4:45 on May 6, Second Corps commander Richard Ewell launched an assault against John Sedgwick's VI Corps. "Ewell's watch must be fifteen minutes ahead of mine," Sedgwick quipped.

"[O]n come the exultant enemy," wrote a member of the 122nd New York, "when we gave them as good a volley as they had just sent, and they sullenly retired a short distance and opened a regular fire upon us." When Federals tried counterattacking, they discovered Ewell's men had significantly strengthened their earthworks overnight—so much so that V Corps commander Gouverneur Warren was too intimidated to pitch in and help Sedgwick despite orders to do so. "[W]e had the enemy entirely in our power and were eager to begin the fray," a Georgian boasted.

"The battle raged furiously all the forenoon, only ceasing long enough for us to close up our depleted ranks," the New Yorker said. "This battle was fought at a terrible disadvantage and with great slaughter on our side."

* * *

To the south, along the Orange Plank Road, Hancock launched his part of the assault just before 5:00 a.m., routing Hill's exhausted and poorly entrenched men with a rush of noise and gunfire. "The roar of musketry, the dying groans of the wounded, the hellish yells of the rebels, and the shouts and cheers of the Union men, mingle together, all making a noise and confusion that is hard to describe," a Michigander said.

As the Confederate line collapsed, Federals pushed through the dense forest in pursuit. "We have to be very

Directed to the point of crisis of May 5 and then ordered to spearhead the assault on May 6, Maj. Gen. Winfield Scott Hancock's II Corps quickly became Grant's go-to soldiers—which would have dire consequences for them as the next six weeks unfolded. The corps started the campaign with nearly 29,000 men but would lose nearly 5,100 of them in the Wilderness. By the middle of June, the corps would suffer more than 16,900 casualties. (loc)

Of Hancock's four division commanders, three were widely regarded as among the best in the entire army: John Gibbon, David Bell Birney, and Francis Barlow (whose division was sketched in action, above). The fourth, Gershom Mott, new to division command, was an unknown. (loc)

careful or we step on their dead and wounded, which lay around in thousands," the Michigander added.

Hancock, exuberant, admired the fine work of his men. "[W]e are driving them most beautifully," he reported. The assault pushed Confederates back more than a mile. Pockets of resistance crumbled; the Federal juggernaut could not be stopped. "The pressure," said a South Carolinian, "was irresistible."

"[I]t looked for awhile that morning as if the last hour of Heth & Wilcox had come," Confederate artillerist Edward Porter Alexander recalled. Grant himself later attested that only the Wilderness itself saved the Confederate army. "[I]f the country has been such that Hancock and his command could have seen the confusion and panic in the lines of the enemy, it would have been taken advantage of so effectually that Lee would not have made another stand outside of his Richmond defenses."

As the Federal push reached the clearing around the Widow Tapp Farm, a row of artillery, perched on a ridge in the field and commanded by Lt. Col. William T. Poague, opened on the blue-clad soldiers. Poague and his cannon—between 12 and 16 of them—were all that stood between the Army of Northern Virginia and utter defeat. "That was, I think the most critical moment which Gen. Lee's fortunes had yet known," Porter said.

Lt. Col. William T. Poague (below) arrayed his guns across Tapp Field as a last-ditch firewall. The guns in Tapp Field today, placed there to represent the Confederate artillery, actually sit west of Poague's true position. (fsnmp)(loc)

Lee tried desperately to rally his infantry. As the usually dependable South Carolinians of Sam McGowan scrambled by, Lee called out to their commander: "My God! Gen. McGowan is that splendid brigade of yours running like a flock of *geese?*"

"No, General!" McGowan answered, stung. "The men are not whipped. They just want a place to form and are ready to fight as well as ever." Lee guided them back into line and threw them back into the fight.

"We hear them forming their broken lines, and their officers lead them forward again," a Federal recalled. "About this time both armies . . . keep up a rattle of musketry like the boiling cauldron of hell. . . ."

Just as the crisis peaked, James Longstreet's men swept onto the field.

* * *

When Lee first started his move toward the Wilderness on May 4, Longstreet had the farthest to march to get to the battlefield. After battle erupted on May 5, no one bothered to tell the First Corps commander about the urgency of the situation unfolding in the Wilderness, so Longstreet took the standard protocol for marching: 50 minutes on the move, 10 minutes rest. Even so, by sundown on May 5, his men had marched an impressive 36 miles in two days. As evening set in, he ordered his column to fall out near Richard's Shop, some 10 miles shy of the battlefield.

Shortly thereafter, a stream of messengers from Lee began arriving, alerting Longstreet to the unfolding crisis. By 1 a.m., he roused his men and again pushed them forward, cutting cross country through the dark in attempt to save time—"the march being difficult and slow in the dense forest by side tracks and deep furrowed roadways," one of his staffers recalled.

Old Pete led them onward, making the Orange

"Lee to the rear!" (fsnmp)

Plank Road and then pushing eastward, doubling them up so he could bring as many of them onto the field at once as he could. As dawn broke, they appeared on the western edge of Tapp Field even as Confederate resistance against Hancock reached its breaking point. "The instant the head of his column was seen, the cries resounded on every side, 'Here's Longstreet. The old War Horse is up at last. It's all right now,'" remembered one private.

Lee, seeing the new arrivals, inquired, "Who are you, my boys?"

"Texas boys!" the men shouted back.

"I am glad to see it," Lee replied. He helped direct the men into position, then prepared to personally lead them into battle.

"Lee to the rear!" the men began to cry. "We won't go on unless you go back!"

Lee resisted, and then only begrudgingly acceded to their wishes. As he moved away, the men of the Lone Star State rushed forward. "Texans always move them!" Lee said admiringly.

The cost to the Texans would be high: they would lose almost two-thirds of their strength moving back the Federal advance.

The rest of Longstreet's men formed up and pushed into battle after the Texans. "Just as we got to the place to file to the right to form a line of battle at right angles with the plank road, the sun rose up appearing in the center of the wood and was as red as a ball of fire," recalled a member of Anderson's brigade.

The Confederate crisis on the Orange Plank Road

had been averted by Longstreet's nick-of-time arrival—
much as the Federal crisis had been averted the previous
day by the similar nick-of-time arrival of Getty's troops.
"Longstreet, always grand in battle, never shone as
he did here," remembered John C. Haskell, one of
Longstreet's artillerymen.

For Lee, though, a different sort of calamity
loomed—one that would certainly tip the balance against
him and his army in the months to come.

And the calamity would feel hauntingly familiar.

At Widow Tapp Field (Stop 9—Southwest Corner)

A walking trail leads from an old parking area out
to a pair of guns that represent William Poague's battery.
The cannon are placed about 200 yards too far back
from their actual position, though, which would have put
them farther out toward the middle of the field.

Just beyond the cannon, the
trail forks. To the left, it runs down
to the site of the Widow Tapp's
house, which had a "companion
corn-crib and log stable . . . partly
masked by meagre plum and cherry
trees. . . ." The house survived the
battle and stood until sometime after
1865. After its demise, the family
constructed two other houses on the
property; the capped well for one
of them still sits beneath a wooden
platform along the right branch of
the walking trail.

That right branch arrows all the way to a set of
earthworks that bisects the field. Brigadier General Joseph
Davis's brigade, held back in reserve from the rest of Heth's
line, occupied this area as support for Poague's guns.

As the works run toward the Orange Plank Road,
the path comes to a clearing where a trio of monuments
commemorates arguably the most storied episode
of the Wilderness: As Lee tried to lead the Texans of
Longstreet's First Corps into battle, they refused, crying
"Lee to the rear!" The event has become a popular
staple of Confederate history, in part because renowned
Southern historian Douglas Southall Freeman helped
purchase some of the land *and* enshrine the story. Three
markers commemorate the event.

The first was installed sometime around September
1891: a quartz bolder placed there by locals to

**The Tapp cabin survived the
battle but later burned down.
The family rebuilt—twice—
closer to the road. Today,
a boarded-over well cap is
all that remains on the site,
tucked among some trees
just to the right of the walking
path.** (cm)

The "Lee to the Rear" marker sits invitingly close to the roadside for passers-by to see, but there's no safe parking in the immediate area for admirers to stop. (cm)

commemorate the Lee-to-the-rear incident. The graves of some 40 Texans killed in battle were located in the area. The bodies were later moved to the Confederate cemetery in Fredericksburg, but the indentations of the graves, and the quartz bolder, are still visible.

Reserve earthworks built after Confederates reestablished their hold along the Orange Plank Road. (cm)

The second monument was erected in August of 1903, supervised by James Power Smith as part of a project to install 10 such stones at key spots on the area's battlefields to commemorate significant Confederate events. At a cost of $25, the granite marker weighs approximately one ton. Its inscription reads, "Lee to the Rear Cried the Texans."

The Texas State Civil War Centennial Commission installed the final marker. The red-granite tablet, which stands eight feet tall and cost about $1,000, tells the "Lee to the Rear" story in much greater—and much more romanticized—detail than the Smith marker. "From this spot the Texas Brigade pleaded with General Lee not to expose himself to Federal fire," it begins:

To commemorate the Civil War Centennial, the state of Texas erected identical red granite memorials at 10 battlefields: Antietam, Bentonville, Chickamauga, Fort Donelson, Gettysburg, Kennesaw Mountain, Mansfield, Pea Ridge, Shiloh, and the Wilderness. (cm)

"WHO ARE YOU MY BOYS?" LEE CRIED AS HE SAW THEM GATHERING.

"TEXAS BOYS," THEY YELLED, THEIR NUMBER MULTIPLYING EVERY SECOND.

THE TEXANS--HOOD'S TEXANS, OF LONGSTREET'S CORPS, JUST AT THE RIGHT PLACE AND THE RIGHT MOMENT! AFTER THE STRAIN OF THE DAWN, THE SIGHT OF THESE GRENADIER GUARDS OF THE SOUTH WAS TOO MUCH FOR LEE. FOR ONCE THE DIGNITY OF THE COMMANDING GENERAL WAS SHATTERED; FOR ONCE HIS POISE WAS SHAKEN.

"HURRAH FOR TEXAS," HE SHOUTED WAVING HIS HAT; "HURRAH FOR TEXAS."

. . . THE WILLING VETERANS SPRANG INTO POSITION....HE WOULD LEAD THEM IN THE COUNTERCHARGE . . . HE SPURRED . . . TRAVELLER . . . ON THE HEELS OF THE INFANTRY MEN.

..."GO BACK, GENERAL LEE, GO BACK!" THEY CRIED "WE WON'T GO ON UNLESS YOU GO BACK!"

Horror in the Forest
CHAPTER ELEVEN
MAY 5-7, 1864

"Danger is far less formidable in the bright, open, ventilated field, than in the dark, close wood," wrote J.F.J. Caldwell, an infantryman from South Carolina; "and it is the experience of every Confederate soldier that we fought more cheerfully where we could see our enemies, were they never so numerous, than where they could creep upon us and deal their blows invisible."

That dread, that creeping dread, lurked everywhere in the Wilderness, a terrible landscape that oppressed soldiers from both sides. The thickets grew so dense "that it was next to impossible to force one's way through them without the loss of cap and tearing of clothing," said a Union soldier from Massachusetts.

Marshes, often hidden, haunted the low spots of the terrain and sucked at the living and the dead alike. "The great, dark woods are filled with dead and wounded from both sides," wrote John Haley of the 17th Maine. "Blue and Gray sink side-by-side in its gloomy thickets and slimy pools."

Soldiers never knew when they'd stumble across a body or stumble into the enemy. Many had trouble just staying in contact with the men to the left and right of them. "The density of the woods rendered it impossible to maintain a regular line of battle," said a captain from Pennsylvania, "so we commenced bushwacking with the enemy on a grand scale." Another soldier likened it to "Indian warfare."

In that fashion, infantryman John McClure of the 14th Indiana found himself in a deadly game of cat-and-mouse with a Confederate. "I hid behind a tree and looked out," McClure wrote. "Across the way…was a rebel aiming at me. I put my hat on a stick . . . and stuck it out

The horrors of the Wilderness loom large in Civil War memory. (cm)

Soldiers from both sides worked together to save wounded men from the spreading fires. (fsnmp)

from behind the tree—as bait. Then I saw him peep out of the thicket and I shot him." McClure, a veteran used to fighting and killing, wasn't so used to experiencing it so intimately. "It was the first time I'd ever seen the man I'd killed, and it was an awful feeling," he said.

Men did things under those trying circumstances they otherwise wouldn't have imagined. One soldier in the 11th New Hampshire saw a group of Confederates build a line of fortifications out of dead bodies: They "would lay a pile of dead men along then dig a trench and throw the dirt over the bodies serving the double purpose of burying their dead and building breastworks."

All around them battle raged, but many men could only tell by the sounds that roared around them, not by anything they could see. "[S]moke clouded the vision, and a heavy sky obscured the sun. . ." wrote Grant's aide, Horace Porter. "It was the sense of sound and of touch rather than the sense of sight which guided the movements. It was a battle fought with the ear, and not with the eye."

"The rattle of musketry would swell into a continuous roar as the simultaneous discharge of 10,000 guns mingled in one grand concert, and then after a few minutes, became more interrupted, resembling the crash of some huge king of the forest when felled by the stroke of the woodsman's ax," wrote a New Yorker. "Then would be heard the wild yells which always told of a rebel charge, and again the volleys would swell into one continuous roll of sound, which would presently be interrupted by the vigorous manly cheers of the northern soldiers . . . which indicated a repulse of their enemies."

Sounds of chaos echoed everywhere. "I could almost hear the confusion of contending armies," wrote William Randall of the 1st Michigan Sharpshooters. "I could almost hear the shrieks of the wounded & the dying, the picture of upturned faces pale and motionless, sleeping their last sleep amid the roar of battle. . . . There was something horrible about this wholesale slaughter of man by man. I could hardly realize that a great battle was raging within a short distance from me."

"This is the raggedest hole I about ever saw," groused Dr. David Holt,

Imagine the fire sweeping up on you faster than you could crawl away. (fsnmp)

tending the wounded of his regiment, the 121st New York, instead of being stationed at a field hospital in the rear. "No wonder we cannot find or see a reb until we get right upon them. Swampy, hilly, bushes thick as dog hair, grape vines, rotten logs and fallen trees, make up this pretty picture. A fine place to fight in surely: a perfect quag mire."

The chaos came in many shapes. One Pennsylvanian had a snake drop on him from a cedar tree. "The sergent jumped and scampered around in much fright paying no attention to the Bullets," a witness said. "The snake took to the grass and di(s)appeared from view. The Sergent thought he could stand a few bullets, but when they commenced shooting Snakes it was time to Stampede."

Sometimes the surprises were far, far worse. "I had dismounted to fix my horse's bit, when a cannonball took off the head of a Jerseyman," recounted Thomas Hyde of Sedgwick's staff;

> *the head struck me, and I was knocked down, covered with brains and blood. Even my mouth, probably gaping in wonder where that shell would strike, was filled, and everybody thought it was all over with me. I looked up and saw the general give me a sorrowful glance, two or three friends dismounted to pick me up, when I found I could get up myself, but I was not much use as a staff officer for fully fifteen minutes.*

Worst of all, perhaps, were the fires. Though the forest itself was lush and green, the dead leaves and detritus of the previous autumn lay ankle deep on the forest floor. Sparks from gunfire set the woods ablaze in a dozen places. "Hundreds of wounded on both sides, unable to crawl away from the swiftly approaching flames, could only lay and moan and roast and die," recalled Maj. Wesley Brainerd of the 50th New York Engineers. "Between the lines, said another Union soldier, "these fires spread unchecked over acres, disfiguring beyond possibility of recognition the bodies of the killed and proving fatal to hundreds of helpless wounded men who lay there looking for the friendly aid which never came and who died at last the victims of the relentless flames."

Cartridge boxes still strapped to the dead and wounded exploded in the flames, blowing "ghastly holes" in the bellies and sides of bodies. "The almost

Field hospitals sprung up in the rears of both armies. The thickness of the brush and the roads clogged with battle made it difficult to evacuate the wounded, though. (fsnmp)

cheerful 'Pop! Pop!' of cartridges gave no hint of the almost dreadful horror their noise bespoke," said a New York Zouave. "The bodies of the dead were blackened and burned beyond all possibility of recognition."

One artillerist saw a soldier with two broken legs "lying on the ground with his cocked rifle by his side and his ramrod in his hand, and his eyes set on the front. I know he meant to kill himself in case of fire—knew it as surely as though I could read his thoughts."

"To add to the miseries of the battle," Brainerd recalled, "no water could be found as no springs or running brooks were in the Wilderness. Many died from thirst, many from excitement and sun-stroke."

And so, as war raged, so did the fires—the smoke from the fight comingling with the smoke from the flames. "The smoke from the clouds of powder and the denser clouds caused by the burning woods became stifling, suffocating, blinding," the engineer said. "Two hundred thousand men, inspired with the desperation of demons, were fighting in a wilderness of fire."

The wounded who could move fought their way through the Wilderness to the rear. "[A] continued stream of faint and bleeding humanity was pouring back from the reeking front, staining the fresh young blades of grass into torrents of blood," said a member of the 11th Pennsylvania, Phil Faulk. Federals had established their field hospitals near Ellwood, at Wilderness Tavern and near the intersection of the Germanna Plank Road and Orange Turnpike. Confederates had established hospitals near Parker's Store along the Orange Plank Road and near Locust Grove and Robinson's Tavern along the Orange Turnpike. Surgeons of both armies worked desperately to save as many as they could. They made "a ghastly sight indeed!" said Meade's aide, Theodore Lyman. "Arms & legs lay outside the operating tents, and each table had a bleeding man on it, insensible from ether and with the surgeons at work on him."

Faulk, getting ready to go under the knife himself, recalled: "Amputating tables groaned with fainting sufferers and the surgeon's knife was plied unceasingly. The scene was sickening and terrible, even as much so as the awful carnage of battle which still raged on like a carnival of hell not two miles distant."

Only a year earlier, these same two armies had fought through this same Wilderness during the battle of Chancellorsville. On the third day of that battle, a portion of the woods had even caught fire. But the close-quarters dread of the Wilderness seemed to overshadow the earlier fight. It was like fighting "in the shadow of death," said one officer.

And whereas the armies at Chancellorsville fought intensely then disengaged, the Wilderness served as the opening of a brawl that would last all summer and cover hundreds of miles. "The campaign is the severest one ever endured by any army in the world," said one officer in the 139th Pennsylvania. Plenty of men on both sides agreed with him. Grant himself later described it as "as desperate fighting as the world has ever witnessed."

"A soldier I once met asked me where I was wounded," recalled Col. Selden Connor of Maine years after the war, "and on my replying 'In the Wilderness' he responded 'Humph! Anybody could get hit there.'"

⟶ **TO STOP 10**

From the Tapp Field parking area, exit left onto Orange Plank Road. In 0.4 miles, you will pass the marker for Col. James Nance on the right. In another 0.2 miles (0.6 miles after leaving the parking area), you will pass the monument for Brig. Gen. James Wadsworth on the left. In another 0.3 miles (0.9 miles after leaving the parking area), you will come to the site of James Longstreet's wounding. Park on the right. Remain there for the next two chapters.

GPS: N 38.29763, W 77.71459

Confederates Unleashed

CHAPTER TWELVE
MAY 6, 1864—AFTERNOON

The memorial to Brig. Gen. James Wadsworth was erected by his grandson, New York Congressman James Wadsworth, in the late fall of 1937. Visiting the battlefield, the Congressman was disappointed by what he considered to be inadequate marking of the spot by the Park Service. He then squabbled with the park's superintendent about the placement of the monument, which is slightly west of the actual spot of Wadsworth's wounding. (cm)

It had all gone so well, and then it had all gone so wrong. Seizing the initiative by attacking first, just before dawn, the Federals had rolled back the entire right wing of the Confederate army. Then, the sudden appearance of the Confederate First Corps knocked the assault back on its heels. Federals stubbornly resisted, but James Longstreet hammered them back, back, back. "Never did his great qualities as a tenacious, fighting soldier shine forth in better light," said his chief of staff, Moxley Sorrel.

By midmorning, Lee received reports that the left end of the Federal line south of the Orange Plank Road was unprotected. Longstreet quickly organized an assault force to move through the forest and along an unfinished railroad cut, then circle around to hit the Union flank.

"It was like an army of ghosts rising out of the earth," one Federal officer recalled. Yet those ghosts hit "[l]ike an avalanche from a mountain side," a Confederate said. First one, then another and another Federal brigade collapsed under the Confederate sweep, which turned the Wilderness into a "vast, weird, horrible slaughter pen." A Vermonter ruefully watched his men fall back around him. "All organization and control seemed to have been lost," he wrote.

As the flanking force swept in, Longstreet executed a perfectly timed frontal assault in concert with it. "Longstreet intended to play his hand for all it was worth, & to push the pursuit with his whole force," remembered Brig. Gen. E. Porter Alexander, Longstreet's chief of artillery.

Federal division commander James Wadsworth, on the Orange Plank Road, tried to staunch the flow of

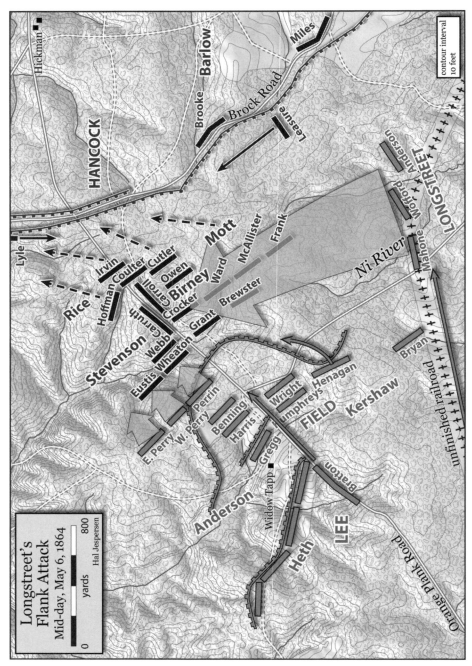

LONGSTREET'S FLANK ATTACK—After blunting Hancock's forward motion, Confederates settled into a stand-up slugging match with them. To break the impasse, Longstreet de-tached several brigades along an abandoned railroad cut for a surprise attack against the Federal left flank. As that attack unfolded, Longstreet launched a powerful frontal assault, too. Federals, unable to withstand the two-front pressure, collapsed.

retreating men while also trying to fend off Longstreet's assault. "[H]e was waving his sword over his head, his silvery hair shining like a meteor's glory," one observer noted. In the mêlée, Wadsworth led a doomed countercharge down the road. "It is certain death," a subordinate proclaimed as Wadsworth ordered his men to follow.

Unable to make headway, Wadsworth ordered his men back. As he did, he lost control of his horse, which bolted toward the Confederates, who shot Wadsworth in the head. For the rest of the afternoon, Confederates traveling the road noticed the white-haired general, propped uncomfortably against a tree along the roadside, barely clinging to life. They rifled through his pockets. Wadsworth would never regain consciousness and died in a Confederate field hospital on May 8. "Thus," said one Federal, "General James S. Wadsworth, the pure patriot, the bravest of the brave, died the soldier's death. . . ."

*   *   *

James Longstreet, too, would meet a grim fate in the Wilderness.

Longstreet rode at the head of a column of fresh troops, advancing toward the newly established Federal position at the Brock Road/Plank Road intersection. One of his staff officers suggested to the general that he was exposing himself too much. "That is our business," Longstreet replied.

Just then elements of the Confederate flanking

Among Wadsworth's V Corps Division was the famed Iron Brigade. May 5 proved to be one of the brigade's worst days of the war; May 6 gave them the chance to again prove their mettle although they would again be forced from the field. Unbeknownst to once-acclaimed unit, the campaign ahead would inflict even more hard times and other disgraces. (loc)

Confederates stripped the wounded James Wadsworth (below) of all his belongings before finally carrying him to a rearward field hospital (bottom), where he lingered in an unconscious stupor. Surgeons unsuccessfully probed his brain to find the bullet lodged there. Dozens of Confederates paraded in and out of his tent to gaze on the millionaire general. "I'd never believe that they had such men as that in their army," one commented. Wadsworth finally died on May 8. (cm)(loc)

column mistook Longstreet's party for Union soldiers and fired upon them. Longstreet took a bullet through the neck and shoulder. Although it didn't kill him, the grievous wound removed him from the fight. (For more on Longstreet's wounding, see Appendix D.)

Longstreet's wounding necessitated a halt in the Confederate advance while officers reorganized, although Longstreet tried to urge them on. "Tell [General Lee]," he said in a choked whisper, "that the enemy were in utter rout, and if pressed, would all be his before night."

A messenger who brought the news to Lee said, "I shall not soon forget the sadness in his face, and the almost despairing movement of his hands, when he was told Longstreet had fallen."

*   *   *

"Could we have pushed forward at once, I believe Grant's army would have been routed," wrote Maj. Gen. Charles Field, the officer who took command in Longstreet's stead. But, Field pointed out, pushing forward at once was impossible. He ordered the flanking force to realign itself with the rest of the Confederate line to prevent further calamities.

It took hours to reorganize, and the delay provided Federals with enough time to construct three lines of breastworks around the intersection. They turned it into "one of the strongest lines of temporary works it had ever been my fortune to stand behind," said a New Yorker.

Despite the loss of his Old War Horse, Lee resolved to maintain the initiative along the Plank Road. Shortly

By the time Lee finally launched the Confederate attack along the Plank Road, Federals had been given four precious hours to fortify and prepare—and even then, it still nearly wasn't enough. (fsnmp)

after 4:00 p.m., he ordered an attack against the Union position. Unfortunately, said a Confederate officer, "it seemed more like an apology for the attack Longstreet was conducting, than anything really calculated to produce results."

The Federals, reorganized and protected by their works, succeeded in repulsing most of the advances, but when the spreading forest fires ignited the logs of the earthworks, it "added renewed terrors and excitement to the situation," said Lt. Josiah M. Favill, a II Corps staff officer. Confederates exploited the opening, charging like "devils through the flames" into the Federal lines.

"The enemy came rushing up to our breastworks, some climbing over them," said Favill. "I saw a rebel officer mount the rampart with a flag in his hand, waving it over the heads of his men. . . . As the rebel flag was flaunting over the burning ramparts, [a] brigade came sweeping up at the double quick, and with a wild hurrah drove the rebels back into the mass of flames

Confederates briefly breached the burning Federal earthworks before being repulsed. (fsnmp)

and smoke and recovered everything that had been temporarily lost."

At that moment, Ambrose Burnside's IX Corps finally appeared on the field in a position to threaten the Confederate left. Confederates countered, but the action effectively ended fighting along the Orange Plank Road.

At Longstreet's Wounding Site

with contributions from
KRISTOPHER D. WHITE

Visitors to Longstreet's wounding site have a 30-minute limit. (cm)

Three parking spaces in a pull-off alongside a busy Orange Plank Road mark the spot where James Longstreet's men accidentally wounded him. The stop not only covers Longstreet's accident, but also informs visitors about the post-battle cemetery placed in the same vicinity (see below).

The site of Stonewall Jackson's wounding, by contrast, is marked by one of the park's two visitor centers. Two monuments, two interpretive trails, a bookstore, a museum, and a movie are dedicated to the man and the battle of Chancellorsville.

Few things better illustrate the dramatically different way Lee's top two lieutenants were treated after the war—and it seemed to go that way right from the beginning.

In 1866, Dr. Hunter Holmes McGuire, Jackson's surgeon, published an account titled "Last Wound of the Late General Stonewall Jackson: The Amputation of the Arm and His Last Moments and Death" in the Richmond Medical Journal. In the years since, it was reprinted numerous times and was even included in Mary Anna Jackson's memoir about her late husband. Today, McGuire's account is still widely available.

Longstreet's medical director, Dr. John Syng Dorsey Cullen—hardly the familiar personality that McGuire became—wrote no account at all of Longstreet's wounding. A few private diarists wrote comments about the first few days of Longstreet's recovery, but several people closely chronicled Jackson's last days—particularly after May 7, when everyone began to realize they were going to be Jackson's last days.

Longstreet's wounding did not take place, as this image suggests, deep in the heart of an ancient forest. (fsnmp)

Between contemporary and modern artists, Jackson's wounding has been painted, sketched, and drawn nearly a dozen times. Longstreet's wounding has been rendered just once—and then, not entirely accurately.

In the early 1900s, James Power Smith, one of Jackson's former aides, returned to the area's battlefields to begin placing a series of 10 granite markers to commemorate key events at key locations. One marker, for instance, marks the location of "Jackson on the field" at Prospect Hill in Fredericksburg. Another marks the location where Jackson's arm was buried at Ellwood. Another sits outside the Stonewall Jackson Shrine at Guiney Station.

At the Wilderness, Smith erected a monument to mark the "Lee to the rear!" incident. That event, Smith must've believed, was the day's most important event because it's the only monument he placed on the actual Wilderness battlefield (aside from one marking the location of Jackson's arm at Ellwood). Longstreet's successful flank attack and his wounding remained unmemorialized.

The spot where Jackson was wounded had two memorials placed there. The first, a giant quartz bolder, was put there sometime between 1876 and 1885. Smith led the effort to erect the second memorial, a pillar of granite blocks almost 15 feet tall, which was dedicated in

Fewer men had more physical control over the story of Longstreet's wounding than former Jackson staff officer James Power Smith. Smith chose what did and did not get enshrined in Confederate memory on the area battlefields. His attachment to Jackson gave extra emphasis to Jackson-related incidents, and elsewhere, he focused on Lee, deeming Longstreet-related stories unimportant enough for commemoration. That tradition, common as part of the Lost Cause interpretation of the war, played out throughout the park's earliest years. For instance, trenches along Lee Drive at Fredericksburg refer to Jackson's corps but Longstreet's individual divisions, making no mention of the corps commander. On Lee Hill, one of Smith's granite markers denotes Lee's HQ on December 13, 1862, but makes no mention of Longstreet, who spent considerable time there with his commander. And of course, at Chancellorsville, Smith helped mark Jackson's wounding with a massive monument while Longstreet's wounding didn't even merit one of Smith's small granite markers. (cm)

June of 1888. The committee that installed it positioned it not to mark the exact spot of Jackson's wounding but rather the general area because they wanted to place it where it would be easily seen from the road.

When the National Park Service built its modern visitors center at Chancellorsville in 1963, it constructed the building to be as close to the wounding site as possible: The wounding spot is less than 30 yards off the northeast corner of the building, giving it special prominence as part of any visitor's experience.

The Park Service gave Longstreet three parking spaces along a road too busy to bring groups of visitors to—with a sign that reads "30-Minute Parking."

Modern scholarship and popular Civil War literature has neglected Longstreet's wounding, too. At least a dozen articles focusing on aspects of Jackson's wounding have been written just in the past 15 years alone. However, with the exception of an excellent article by Robert E. L. Krick, "Like a Duck on a Junebug" (published in Gary Gallagher's 1997 collection of essays, *The Wilderness Campaign*), and an article of questionable merit on "The Cervical Wound of General Longstreet" by a pair of doctors (published in 2000 in a medical journal), there remains little on Longstreet. The May 2009 issue of *America's Civil War* featured an in-depth examination of the event, "Unfriendly Fire," co-authored by Chris Mackowski and Kristopher D. White (see Appendix D).

Certainly Jackson's death—considered by some as martyrdom—lends an air of romance to the story of his wounding that Longstreet's memory would not benefit from. Yet post-war efforts to remember the war's events in a certain way, such as placing an emphasis on Jackson over Longstreet, still influence the way those events are interpreted today. Does Longstreet's wounding get less attention because it was less important, or do modern visitors think Longstreet's wounding was less important because it gets less attention?

Across the road from the parking area is one of the trailheads for the Federal line hiking trail. The other end of the trail comes out at the park's picnic area along Hill-Ewell Drive. It's a 3.7-mile hike to go down and back. Near the Longstreet wounding site, the trail provides an excellent view of the topography, making it easier to understand how Longstreet got caught in the crossfire he did.

Farther down the trail, which winds between housing developments along a thin strip of preserved national park property, the path follows one of the lines of earthworks constructed by the Federals. As the trail nears the Orange Turnpike to the north, hikers can see some of the park's best-preserved earthworks and some

amazing artillery lunettes that marked the southernmost position of the batteries stationed around Ellwood.

Wilderness Cemetery #2 originally sat in the area near the southwest corner of the small parking area here. Established in June 1865 and surrounded by a small white picket fence, the cemetery contained more than 500 burials, 10 men to a grave. All but five were unknown. "It was impossible to identify any of the bodies found unburied," said a member of one burial party. "[T]hey having been exposed [for] more than a year all traces of identification having been destroyed. . . ." The soldiers were reinterred a year later at the Fredericksburg National Cemetery.

Longstreet's wounding site was also the location of Wilderness Cemetery #2. Beginning in 1866, the bodies were disinterred and moved to Fredericksburg National Cemetery. The forest floor throughout this entire section of forest remains pocked with depressions where bodies had once been buried. (loc)(cm)

Gordon's Flank Attack

CHAPTER THIRTEEN

MAY 6, 1864—EVENING

Although fighting had fizzled out along the Orange Turnpike, Lee wasn't finished.

From north of the Orange Turnpike, news arrived that the right flank of the Union army also appeared vulnerable. Gordon, reconnoitering the enemy's position that morning, "ascertained that [the Federal] right flank, resting in a dense woodland, was left unprotected," he later reported, attributing the oversight to the fact that Sedgwick was largely preoccupied by the action that had erupted at 4:15.

Neither Meade nor Grant had apparently learned a lesson about protecting the army's flanks after Longstreet's successful assaults, so Confederates resolved to teach the lesson again.

Gordon pressed for a flanking attack at the northernmost edge of the battlefield, but his immediate supervisor, Maj. Gen. Jubal Early, balked. Gordon's "views were opposed by General Early, who thought the attempt unsafe," Ewell later recounted. "[I]n consequence of this delay and other unavoidable causes, the movement was not begun until nearly sunset."

Gordon launched his attack as dusk settled over the deep woods, which would eventually make it impossible for him to maintain effective communication and coordination. At its outset, though, the attack crushed the Union opposition. "The scene was instantly a very pandemonium of sights and sounds," said one soldier. "The crashing of the timber under the artillery fire, the rolling volleys, the rattling . . . fire, the commands and cheers of our people and the fierce Rebel yell filled the air with sounds, while the hand-to-hand encounters, the clubbed musket and the bayonet were brought into play."

The Gordon Flank Attack Trail parallels several sets of Federal trenches, including the final Federal line along the trail's easternmost leg (left). The trail elsewhere parallels the Confederate works. (cm)

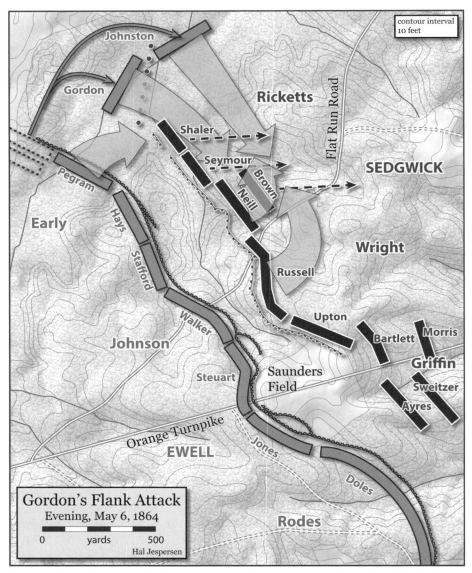

GORDON'S FLANK ATTACK—Brig. Gen. John Brown Gordon advocated for much of the day for an attack against the Union right flank, but his immediate supervisor, division commander Maj. Gen. Jubal Early, argued against it. Much controversy still remains over the sequence of events that led to Gordon finally getting approval from Second Corps commander Richard Ewell, but by the time Gordon launched his assault, he had little daylight left to work with. Darkness as much as Union opposition checked him.

Gordon "attacked vehemently," Ewell said. "Of the force encountered not an organized regiment remained, and nearly all had thrown away their arms."

"Repeated efforts were made by brigade commanders to change front and check our advance,"

Gordon boasted. "These commands were rapidly broken and scattered."

"They swung around to our rear, and we had more than we could take care of," said a New Yorker. The VI Corps fell back, but their commander, Sedgwick, soon rallied them along a narrow road. "Halt! For God's sake, boys, rally!" Sedgwick bellowed. "Don't disgrace yourselves and your general this way!"

In the end, "the approach of darkness in the dense woodland created confusion," Gordon said. Night, more so than Sedgwick's rally, brought the fighting to a sputtering halt.

Word of the Confederate assault reached Grant around the same time darkness brought an end to the fighting. "Had there been daylight," Grant later wrote, "the enemy could have injured us very much in the confusion that prevailed."

This later proved a major source of postwar contention between Gordon and Early, who told differing stories about their disagreement, which led to the delayed start time. "I must be permitted in this connection," Gordon wrote in his official report, "to express the opinion that had the movement been made at an earlier hour and properly supported . . . it would have resulted in a decided disaster to the whole right wing of General Grant's army, if not in its entire organization."

Ewell's account generally agreed with Gordon's,

"That after two . . . combats, worn and fatigued, they should have failed before comparatively fresh troops, will be justly considered as no more than was to be expected," a VI Corps officer said, trying to excuse the collapse of his men. (loc)

Union brigadier generals Alexander Shaler (right) and Truman Seymour (left) both wound up as Confederate prisoners. Seymour said in his official report that the Confederate attack hit with such strength that his line was "rolled up with great rapidity. Portions of the command faced to the rear and held their position for a short time, but were compelled to give way. . . . The right of the line was perfectly unsupported, and of necessity so thin that successful resistance to such a flank attack was at least improbable." (fsnmp)(fsnmp)

although Gordon didn't help his own case because he embellished his side of the story as time went on—as did Early. As a result, the "too little, too late" flank attack remains one of the most intriguing sources of speculation from the battle.

* * *

Thus ended the second day of fighting in the Wilderness.

Grant had sought to push Confederates with a series of strong, coordinated attacks, but Lee upended those plans by exercising the initiative for most of the day—"not because Lee had obviously the best of it," observed one of Grant's staffers, "but because [Grant] himself had discovered the Army of the Potomac's one weakness, the lack of springy formation, and audacious, self-reliant initiative."

It proved to be an invaluable lesson for the general from out west, who would soon demonstrate himself to be a quick learner.

At Gordon's Flank Attack

A trail through this area of the battlefield can be found at Saunders Field. See "At Saunders Field (Stop 4A)" in Chapter 5.

VI Corps commander Maj. Gen. John Sedgwick was so beloved by his men they called him "Uncle John." (loc)

A portion of the fighting along the northern part of the battlefield took place on ground now occupied by a gated community, Lake of the Woods. In 2014, to commemorate the battle's sesquicentennial, the Lake of the Woods Civil War Study Group dedicated a "Monument to the Fallen"—one panel commemorating Northern soldiers and one commemorating Southern soldiers. The monument is located near the corner of the parking lot for the Lake of the Woods Church, in the area where Shaler and Seymour were taken captive. (jh)

→ A NOTE ABOUT THE TOUR

You may, at this point, remain here for the final chapters or return to Stop 8 (the Brock Road/Plank Road intersection). To get to Stop 8, carefully merge back onto the Plank Road and continue east for 0.3 miles. On the way, you'll drive down into the swale where the 12th Virginia Infantry crossed the road (see Appendix D). The parking area for the tour stop will be on the right, just before the intersection.

GPS: N 38.30087, W 77.70938

Additionally, you may wish to visit Todd's Tavern, scene of cavalry fighting on May 7 (see Appendix A). Todd's Tavern was also an important stop on the route to Spotsylvania on the night of May 7-8. From Longstreet's Wounding Site, carefully merge back onto the Plank Road and continue east for 0.3 miles. At the Brock Road/Plank Road intersection, turn right onto Brock Road. Travel 4.8 miles. A pull-off for Todd's Tavern will be on the right, opposite the modern Todd's Tavern convenience store.

GPS: N 38.24763, W 77.66893

$\mathcal{G}$rant Moves $\mathcal{S}$outh

CHAPTER FOURTEEN
MAY 7, 1864

It would not have been an exaggeration to call it the middle of nowhere: an unremarkable crossroads in the heart of the Wilderness where the Orange Plank Road and Brock Road intersected.

By the afternoon of May 5, 1864, it had become the most important intersection in America. For Confederates, the intersection represented an opportunity to wedge themselves between two wings of the Union army, catching them off guard and preventing their unification. For Federals, the intersection represented an opportunity to block an aggressive and unexpected Confederate movement that put the Northern army in jeopardy.

By the night of May 6, however, the crossroads represented far, far more.

Two days of intense fighting and blistering fire had swirled around the intersection, with neither side holding any more advantage than they'd possessed before the battle opened.

"Joe Johnston would have retreated after two days of such punishment," Ulysses S. Grant noted, calling to mind the principal general of the Confederacy's western armies. Johnston would have retreated, but Robert E. Lee kept coming and coming and coming. Lee had, in fact, successfully achieved his primary goal, striking a blow at the Federal army in a spot where the Federal army could not effectively strike back.

But Grant, too, had achieved something important. He had drawn Lee out from behind Confederate fortifications and into battle. The result, although not a tactical victory, represented a strategic one.

The last fighting of May 6 had sputtered into occasional after-dark potshots between pickets. Forest

The Brock Road/Plank Road intersection looks deceptively quiet, but in fact, it remains a busy crossroads because of two large gated communities nearby. On May 7, 1864, the future of the entire war effort hinged on the crossroads Grant came to here. (cm)

fires roared like freight trains and threw orange light and black smoke into the night. Wounded men, lost in the undergrowth, groaned and shrieked and wept. Members of Grant's and Meade's staffs, atop their knoll at the Lacy farm, could see, could hear, could smell the destruction all around them.

Grant himself, deep in thought, stared into his campfire. He wore his hat pulled low over his eyes. He had earlier abandoned his whittling, had gone into his tent to give voice to his grief, had returned with his old stoicism draped across his face to sit by the campfire and contemplate the crossroads before him.

Somewhere nearby, a band began to play. The song, familiar to all, floated down from the Lacy farm and over the battlefield and, said a Confederate, "it re-echoed through that pine forest, the old patriot air, 'The Star Spangled Banner,' and after that music had died away our band responded with that air so dear to Southern hearts, 'The Bonnie Blue Flag,' and it was responded to by 'Home, Sweet Home.'"

That's where the army would be heading soon, many Federals thought—back north, back home, back to safety, away from the indomitable Lee and the Army of Northern Virginia. Federal commanders had all found grief at Lee's hands, and all had withdrawn or, at the very least, had avoided further bludgeoning. Grant, most assumed, would act no differently now that he'd gotten his first taste of what Lee could do. "[H]e is now studying how to get back across the Rapidan," one Union soldier sneered.

*   *   *

As May 7 dawned, surgeons lifted James Longstreet into the back of an ambulance for the trip to Orange Court House, where a train would take him to Charlottesville to begin his long recuperation. "He is very feeble and nervous and suffers much from his wound," said an observer, although the overall prognosis looked favorable.

Lee saw his trusted lieutenant off, then set about the work of deciding upon a replacement. He had several capable officers to choose from, and in the end he settled on Maj. Gen. Richard Anderson—"chivalrous, deliberate 'Dick' Anderson," as one of Longstreet's aides described him. Although not an especially brilliant strategist, Anderson performed solidly enough and was familiar to the men.

As morning passed into afternoon, Lee's men, entrenched in a strong line that snaked through the thick undergrowth, traded shots and forays with their Union counterparts, but Lee, "constrained to spare his men as much as possible, hesitated to assail the enemy in his intrenched [sic] position," said a Confederate officer. Instead, Lee "hopefully awaited attack." Grant had spent the previous two days trying to assume the offensive, and Lee had every reason to think he would do so again. And so Lee waited.

As the day wore on, and it became apparent Grant would not launch the attacks Lee expected, the Confederate commander began to consider the other possibilities that lay before him. If Grant didn't attack, then he would have to move—but in which direction? Retreat back across the Rapidan the way he'd come? Withdraw eastward toward Fredericksburg? Move southward toward Spotsylvania Court House? The options provided Lee with some difficult choices.

To better determine Grant's intentions, Lee sent a pair of reconnaissance forces to the north. He also ordered his engineers to construct a trail through the woods toward the south so he could move to intercept the Federals if they shifted that way.

Confederate soldiers spent the day trying to scavenge what they could from the field. Burial parties interred corpses individually in shallow graves where they fell or sometimes in communal pits the shovellers marked with crude headboards. They searched the bodies of Union dead for money and valuables. One Confederate, who hadn't eaten since before the battle, scavenged for food. "I have been so hungry that I have cut the blood off from crackers and eaten them," he complained.

By mid-afternoon, Lee began to receive reports that Grant might be preparing a move southward, toward Spotsylvania Court House. He asked his cavalry in that direction to gather more intelligence, and he prepped the newly promoted Anderson, who would lead the Confederate withdrawal, on what to do.

For Longstreet's replacement, Lee first leaned toward his "Bad Old Man," Jubal Early, but decided in favor of Maj. Gen. Richard H. Anderson. Anderson had once served in the First Corps prior to the army's reorganization the previous summer, so Lee thought he would be more familiar—and thus more acceptable—to the men. Because of the First Corps's location, it would fall to Anderson to lead the army out of the Wilderness. (loc)

* * *

Indeed, Grant knew he could not stand for more punishment in the Wilderness. "I do not hope to gain any decided advantage from the fighting in this forest," he told an aide. Yet he knew he could not—would not—retreat. As he had told a newspaper correspondent the previous evening, there would be no turning back.

Grant had, by then, already made his choice: a move around Lee's right flank. "This will, in all probability, compel him to try and throw himself between us and Richmond," Grant explained to an aide, "and in such a movement I hope to be able to attack him in a more open country, and outside of his breastworks."

Grant issued his order early on the morning of May 7, stressing the need for secrecy. An uneasy détente

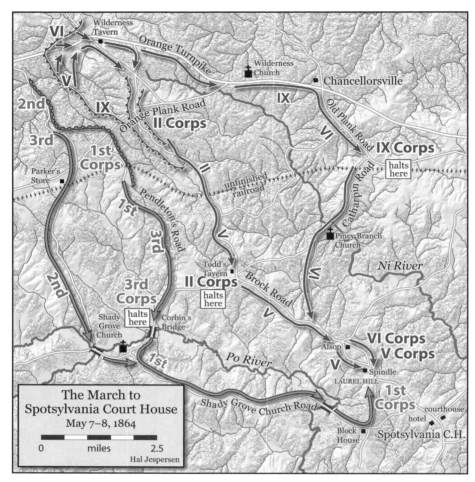

THE MARCH TO SPOTSYLVANIA COURT HOUSE—Grant intended to reach Spotsylvania Court House by 8 a.m. on May 8, 1864. He targeted the village because its road network would give him the inside track to Richmond, which Lee would have to defend. Lee's cavalry delayed Grant's advance, however, giving Confederate infantry time to cover nearly twice the distance and intercept Federals before they reached the village. The subsequent battle of Spotsylvania Court House would last two weeks.

held between the two armies, with skirmishing erupting at various points along the line all day. If Lee divined Grant's intentions, he might bring on a full engagement or slide out of position and look for a way to disrupt Grant's maneuver.

But both sides seemed content to skirmish throughout the day without launching any all-out assaults. Occasionally, artillery opened fire. In the early afternoon, Confederate shells began to rain down around Ellwood. "[T]he enemy's shells fall near . . . Headquarters," complained Warren. Meade, at his own headquarters nearby, snapped a reply: "Well, can't I see

that? What's that to do with it?" He refused to authorize a vigorous response for fear of escalating the conflict even as preparations continued to move the army.

As part of those preparations, surgeons shuttled wounded soldiers to the rear, toward Chancellorsville, and eventually on to Fredericksburg. Supply wagons prepared to move. Cavalry rode forward to scout the way. Burial parties carried out their solemn work. Infantrymen destroyed anything the Confederates might be able to scavenge. "The arms in our possession, either captured from the enemy or belonging to our killed and wounded, were gathered up and broken or buried," said an artillerist; "and in order to deceive the enemy headboards were placed over them containing the names of fictitious soldiers."

Just after dusk, Grant rode out to the Brock Road/Plank Road crossroads. He had faced a crossroads of his own and had chosen to go forward. That road, literally, ran southeast from this intersection, which his men had fought so hard to retain control of. Now, the fruits of their work provided the Army of the Potomac a road to travel onward. This would be no McClellan-esque "On to Richmond!" drive full of pomp and bluster—but soldiers along the road did notice which direction Grant was moving as he and his staff trotted past them:

By the afternoon of May 7, the II Corps had well fortified its position along the Brock Road (top). The logworks have since decayed and caved in on themselves, leaving little more than a small hump of dirt and a shallow ditch (bottom). (fsnmp)(cm)

"[T]he chief who had led them through the mazes of the Wilderness was again moving forward with his horse's head turned toward Richmond."

Their reaction was as spontaneous as it was exuberant. "Soldiers weary and sleepy after their long battle, with stiffened limbs and smarting wounds, now sprang to their feet, forgetful of their pains, and rushed forward to the roadside," wrote Porter. "Wild cheers echoed through the forest, and glad shouts of triumph rent the air. Men swung their hats, tossed up their arms, and pressed forward to within touch of their chief, clapping their hands, and speaking to him with the familiarity of comrades."

Staffers urged the men to keep quiet to preserve the secrecy Grant wanted to maintain. "[B]ut," Porter added, "the demonstration did not really cease until the general was out of sight."

The Army of the Potomac, for the first time in its career, was moving forward after a battle.

* * *

Lee had caught the move, and although Grant had a head start, Lee had a smaller, faster army. Anticipating the possible need to maneuver out of the Wilderness, Lee ordered artillery chief William Pendleton to cut a road southward through the dark, close wood that would provide an avenue of escape. By nightfall, the Army of Northern Virginia was on the move—spurred on as much by the need to escape the burning forest as to get the jump on Grant.

The race southward was on.

Todd's Tavern sat along the road to Spotsylvania Court House. Meade ordered his cavalry to clear the road and secure the area in preparation for the army's advance in that direction. (fsnmp)

"Such were the prominent features of the entire campaign," wrote a Confederate artillerist. "It was a succession of death grapples and recoils and races for new position, and several times during the campaign the race was so close and tense and clearly defined that we could determine the exact location of the Federal column by the cloud of dust that overhung and crept along the horizon parallel to our own advance."

With the help of his cavalry, Lee managed to slip ahead of Grant and dictate terms of battle. "In his renewed effort to get past our flank," wrote a Confederate officer admiringly, "Grant gave us further experience of his qualities as a general."

From the crossroads in the Wilderness, Grant would move his army left and to the south, left and to the south, fighting Lee whenever he could bring on an engagement, flanking him when he couldn't. "I propose to fight it out along this line if it takes all summer," Grant would declare.

That line, left and to the south, would take the armies to the outskirts of Spotsylvania Courthouse, to the steep banks of the North Anna River and to Totopotomoy Creek, and to the killing grounds of Cold Harbor. Then Grant would swing south of the James River and settle into a siege around Petersburg. And all the time, he would hold to his original plan: "to hammer continuously against the armed force of the enemy and his resources, until by mere attrition, if in no other way, there should be nothing left to him."

Joshua Lawrence Chamberlain, an officer from Maine, would later observe: "The hammering

The II Corps's works extended as far along Brock Road as the intersection with Jackson Trail West, which the works then parallel for another half a mile. (cm)

For years afterwards, travelers passing through the Wilderness saw grim reminders of the battle still scattered across the landscape. (fsnmp)

business had been hard on the hammer." Grant left in his wake some 18,000 casualties in the Wilderness alone, compared to some 11,000-13,000 Confederate casualties. The names of the dead began to appear in long rolls on the front pages of newspapers, and as the Overland Campaign ground onward, Northern morale sank ever deeper and cries for an end to the war grew louder. Morale sank so low President Lincoln felt assured he would fail in his reelection bid—making himself a casualty of that same grim math he knew was necessary to win the war.

But once Grant made his choice at the crossroads in the Wilderness, once he resolved to take the road southward, direction would never again matter. It would only be a matter of time before the road led to Appomattox Court House.

OPPOSITE: At the Brock Road/ Plank Road intersection, a bronze compass points the way toward Spotsylvania Court House, the next stop on the bloody campaign trail. (cm)

Epilogue

The salmon-colored house on the crest of the hill at the heart of the Lacy plantation, Ellwood, stood vacant for eight years after the war ended. Surviving records suggest the house remained uninhabitable for a time and that the Lacys then rented out the farm for a spell. A carpetbagger, hoping in vain that the property would be confiscated, may have squatted in the building for a time, too.

But by 1872, after selling their grand home, Chatham, to settle debts, the Lacys moved from Fredericksburg to take up permanent residence in their country estate. Only two of their former slaves remained with them.

Despite the postwar depression that afflicted the South, the Lacys once again transformed their farm into a profitable enterprise.

Two newspaper correspondents, traveling across Virginia in the summer of 1879, paid a visit to Ellwood at Lacy's invitation. The land they found hardly resembled the dark, close wood of the war years. "We saw nothing particularly 'wild,' 'weird,' or 'howling,' about the Wilderness," they wrote:

> It was not the most interesting country, to be sure. But the blackberries were the finest we had eaten, the green apples the sourest; the houses were whitewashed and neatly kept; flowers were tenderly reared by even the poorest and plainest of the people...the roads good; and all things wearing a thrifty, peaceful, and happy aspect . . . .

> Here in the autonomy of Ellwood, situated in a beautiful valley and extending in some directions as far as the eye could reach, our genial host entertained us in a way that . . . would never associate with the 'weird shadows and the awful gloom' of the Wilderness.

After May 1864, Ellwood would never again see the hard hand of war, but it would still see hard times aplenty. (fsnmp)

Two years earlier, in 1877, the unfinished railroad that ran between Fredericksburg and Orange Court House had finally been completed. The train traveling the narrow-gauge line stopped in the hamlet of Parker's Store—although, by that time, the store itself was no more. Two other general stores sprang up in the area, though, along with a post office, a wagon shop, and a pair of lumber dealers.

Nearby, the Widow Tapp and her family settled into new quarters. Their cabin survived the battle but was mysteriously destroyed in 1865. A second cabin built in the same location was also destroyed years later. Each time, the family rebuilt.

Another widow, Permelia Higgerson, remarried in 1867, but she would find little happiness in her postwar life. She and her new husband, Daniel Porter, had two children, but the youngest, a daughter, died as a teenager. Daniel, meanwhile, had an affair with his stepdaughter, Jacqueline. When Jacqueline eventually became pregnant, she and her stepfather ran off together to Missouri. Permelia, left behind,

Ellwood has gone through many iterations over the years: 1963 (top) and 1978 (bottom). (fsnmp)(fsnmp)

watched as the first of Daniel's children passed away, leaving behind two boys of his own. Their grandmother took them in.

Meanwhile, Permelia's brother, Absalom, tried for years on his mother's behalf to get compensation from the United States government for the damage done to their home at Mount View and the property stolen from the farm. In 1875, Absalom's mother died, although Absalom continued to pursue the case, which was finally denied. Absalom eventually gave up and remodeled the farmhouse on his own in 1891, and he lived there until his death in 1923. His former slave, Thorton, lived at Mount View, too, until his death sometime in the 1880s.

Absalom's family, which occupied Mount View until it burned down in 1947, continued to find artifacts from the war strewn across the property. Some leftovers were less innocuous than others: Parts of the Chewning farm remained off limits for years because of unexploded ordinance.

War of a kind returned to the Wilderness in the fall

President Warren G. Harding talks with local Confederate veteran Judge John Goolrick while Marine General Smedley Butler looks on. Also in attendance at the training exercises was Assistant Secretary of the Navy Theodore Roosevelt, Jr. (fsnmp)

of 1921. More than 4,000 Marines marched into the area for a four-day training exercise. Under the command of Gen. Smedley Butler, the Marines outlined an imaginary battleship in the Wilderness Run valley, then used their planes and anti-aircraft guns and nighttime searchlights to "defend" the ship. President Warren Harding attended the event.

By then, life at nearby Ellwood had dramatically slowed. The Lacys had moved out of the big house, back to Fredericksburg, in the 1890s. In 1907, their children sold the property to Hugh Evander Willis, a respected legal scholar. Willis's family lived at Ellwood until 1977, when they turned the property over to the National Park Service.

But perhaps the real end of the postwar era came in June 1944. One of the Wilderness's oldest residents, the last-known civilian who survived the great battle of May 1864—4-year-old Eliza "Phenie" Tapp—died at the age of 84, just days before Allied forces stormed the beaches of Normandy in another, very different war. "Her death marks the removal of one more link with the past," her obituary read; "one more living being who walked the same roads that Lee and Longstreet and Meade and Grant trod is now gone.

"She saw the same violets and bluets in that wood of death that the soldiers trampled underfoot and spattered with their blood. Now she and the soldiers are gone, but the flowers are the same every May, still blooming along the dusty 'plank' road and on the grass-covered trenches, while the adversaries of that battlefield, reincarnate in their descendants of a new century, fight now side by side."

"Their Spencer Carbines Made the Dense Woods Ring"

Federal Cavalry in the Battle of the Wilderness

APPENDIX A

BY DANIEL T. DAVIS

A group of riders quietly made their way along the road toward the river. As they neared the bank, they came to a halt. Final instructions were whispered, equipment secured, and pistols readied. Around early dawn on the morning of May 4, 1864, the small force splashed through the water and up the opposite side. The Confederate pickets on guard rapidly scattered. Quite easily, Brig. Gen. James H. Wilson's cavalry division secured Germanna Ford on the Rapidan River. "The rising sun shone upon its flags," a New Yorker remembered, "already borne over earthworks which the enemy had used on former occasions."

Wilson was the vanguard of the Army of the Potomac as it opened the spring campaign. His assignment was twofold: screen the infantry as it marched into the second-growth forest known as the Wilderness and give advance warning of any Confederate activity. For the inexperienced Wilson, it was a heavy assignment.

Prior to the spring of 1864, Wilson had served primarily in staff positions, first for Maj. Gen. George McClellan and then later for Maj. Gen. Ulysses S. Grant. Promoted to brigadier general in the fall of 1863, Wilson was assigned to the Cavalry Bureau the following February. A favorite of Grant's, Wilson left his desk duties less than two months later. Recently promoted to lieutenant general, Grant assigned Wilson to lead the Third Cavalry Division in the Army of the Potomac. It was his first field command with the mounted arm.

As Wilson's troopers fanned out along the heights above the river, Federal engineers assembled a bridge for the approaching infantry and wagons. Once the lead elements of the V Corps came into view, Wilson struck out along the Germanna Plank Road toward Wilderness Tavern. From there, he sent scouting parties westward along the Orange Turnpike in the direction of the Confederates. When the Union infantry arrived, Wilson

The Wilderness was not a hospitable environment for horsemen. Today, horses are allowed only on the shoulders of park roads, on the Gordon Flank Attack Trail between tour stops 2 and 3, and on a maintenance access road in the Gordon Flank Attack area.
For more information, contact the park's Office of Law Enforcement. (cm)

continued south to a place called Parker's Store on the Orange Plank Road. In the process, he left the turnpike unguarded. When he reached Parker's Store, Wilson detailed Col. John Hammond's 5th New York Cavalry to cover the thoroughfare as the rest of the division bedded down for the evening.

The Catharpin Road bisected the Brock Road at Todd's Tavern. Both Confederates and Federals made use of this second axis of advance as they sparred on May 7. (fsnmp)

Apprised of the enemy movement, Gen. Robert E. Lee had set his army in motion toward the Federals. That night, lead elements of Lt. Gen. Richard Ewell's Second Corps stopped along the Orange Turnpike. Before them lay an open route toward the Union army.

On the morning of May 5, Wilson saddled up to continue his screen of the blue infantry. Leaving Hammond in place, he set out with the rest of his command in the direction of Craig's Meeting House along the Catharpin Road. Shortly after his departure, Confederate infantry from Lt. Gen. A.P. Hill's Third Corps, coming down the Plank Road, surprised Hammond's pickets. Sending word back to army headquarters, Hammond prepared to defend his position.

Hill was not the only surprise the Federals received that morning, though. Shortly after Hammond's dispatch, Ewell's infantry was spotted along the turnpike.

As the Federal high command dispatched infantry to the Orange Plank Road, the New Yorkers put up a stubborn resistance against the mounting Confederate pressure. "Fighting with a daring rarely equaled," one of his troopers wrote, "and compelled to fall back before superior numbers, we nevertheless held them at bay for five hours." Fortunately for Hammond, Brig. Gen. George Getty's VI Corps division later arrived to relieve them and solidify the Union position along the Orange Plank Road.

Meanwhile, Wilson continued his march, unaware of the developing battle he had left behind. He was also in for a shock of his own, however, when his pickets encountered Confederate cavalry led by Brig. Gen. Thomas Rosser. The two sides collided along an old farm trace above the Catharpin Road. "The action was on at once and, as both sides were anxious to gain the first advantage, it soon became furious," Wilson wrote.

"With a Rebel yell," one of Rosser's men recalled, the Confederates charged Wilson's line. "For a while they stood firm and received the charge. Now it was man-to-

Daniel T. Davis, *education manager at the American Battlefield Trust, is an emeritus member of Emerging Civil War. He is the author of several books and an authority on Eastern Theater cavalry actions.*

man and hand-to-hand. Pistol and sabre were busy in slaughter, while the shrieks of the stricken and the shouts of the victors mingled with the roar of battle."

At first, Wilson stood firm, but then his line began to give way under Rosser's assault. Although he was able to pull away from the Confederates, Wilson soon learned they were moving parallel to his column in an attempt to flank him. Threatened with being cut off, Wilson sent his troopers galloping along the lane. Fortunately, he was able to reach the safety of Brig. Gen. David Gregg's division at Todd's Tavern.

Wilson did not participate in any fighting for the remainder of the battle. Early the following day, he withdrew his tired and hard-fought troopers to the vicinity of Chancellorsville to rest and refit.

Wilson failed his first test as a field commander. He left the Orange Turnpike completely open for Ewell's infantry to surprise the Yankees and was nearly surrounded during his engagement with Rosser. Wilson's failure was, in fact, the failure of his commanding officer, cavalry chief Maj. Gen. Philip Sheridan, who put a rookie at the lead of the army and then didn't monitor the situation.

Wilson's difficulty in the Wilderness did allow him to mature as an officer. In the autumn of 1864, he was given command of the cavalry of the Military Division of the Mississippi. There, he put his administrative and combat skills to good use. His reorganization and guiding hand proved vital to the men in his charge. Wilson's troopers played a critical role in the Union victory at Nashville, which secured Tennessee for the Federals. In the spring of 1865, Wilson led a massive cavalry raid through Alabama and Georgia. He later served as a major general in the Spanish American War and in the Boxer Rebellion. Wilson passed away in Wilmington, Delaware, on February 23, 1925.

Aside from Wilson's misadventure, the rest of the Federal cavalry would continue to tussle with their Confederate counterparts mostly along the Brock Road in the vicinity of Todd's Tavern. There, on the southeast edge of the Wilderness, the country opened up a bit. Grant charged Sheridan with protecting the Federal left flank and keeping the road clear to Spotsylvania Courthouse. Fighting erupted there around 4:00 p.m. on May 7 and lasted until after dark, when Confederates withdrew. Sheridan, content to not pursue, held the crossroads by the tavern while Confederates blocked Brock Road to the south and Catharpin Road to the west. This, Sheridan's failure, would allow Confederates to win the race to Spotsylvania Courthouse later that night, as the Overland Campaign shifted into its next deadly phase.

James Wilson had earned Grant's trust through solid performances in the Western Theater. Grant thought highly enough of his young protégé that he brought Wilson east with him for the spring campaign. (loc)

Phil Sheridan would try to compensate for his failure at Todd's Tavern by riding off with the entire cavalry corps—a move Grant would authorize over Meade's objections—leaving the army without its eyes and ears. (loc)

"It's Griffin, not Gregg":
Cracks in the Army of the Potomac's High Command

APPENDIX B
BY RYAN QUINT

A very angry Brig. Gen. Charles Griffin, trailed by one of his staff officers, rode up to the Army of the Potomac's command center around 2:45 p.m. on May 5, 1864. Dismounting, Griffin's "face was stern and flushed," as Lt. Col. Theodore Lyman remembered. Standing among the combined staffs of his superiors, Maj. Gen. George Meade and Lt. Gen. Ulysses S. Grant, Griffin began to scream.

Lyman narrated Griffin's tirade in his personal diary: "Says in a loud voice that he drove the enemy. . . ¾ of a mile, but got no support on the flanks, and had to retreat . . . . Implies censure on [Brig. Gen. Horatio] Wright and apparently on his corps commander, [Maj. Gen. G.K.] Warren."

In the wake of Griffin's yelling, as if a hurricane had just rolled through, stood the shocked members of Grant's entourage, including his chief of staff, John Rawlins. He thought Griffin's actions in front of his superiors was "mutinous and wished him put in arrest."

Grant, in his first battle as the new general-in-chief of the United States Army and still getting familiar with the machinations of the Army of the Potomac, thought the same thing. Looking to Meade, Grant asked incredibly, "Who is this Gen. *Gregg?* You ought to arrest him!"

In response, Meade the Old Snapping Turtle, noticing Grant's buttons unfastened, reached out and "began to button it up, as if he were a little boy, saying in a good-natured voice, 'It's 'Griffin,' not 'Gregg,' and it's only his way of talking.'"

And that was it—there is nothing else included about what happened in response to Griffin's outburst in the wake of his failed attack at Saunders Field. However, even the facts included allow remarkable understanding into the command status of the Army of the Potomac in the opening days of the Overland Campaign.

Before the campaign got underway and Grant decided to make his headquarters in the field with the Army of the Potomac, there was a flawed perception such a setup would work—Grant

Grant "seems not at all disposed to interfere with my army in any details," Meade surmised in late March. The Overland Campaign would prove him wrong. As the campaign unfolded, Grant took a heavier and heavier hand directing the Army of the Potomac. (fsnmp)

Artist Alfred Waud sketched Grant and Meade visiting Warren at the Lacy house. (loc)

Although he made a less-than-stellar first impression on Grant, Charles Griffin would eventually rise to command at the corps level, taking over the V Corps in the final days of the war. (fsnmp)

in overall command of the entire Federal army, but still allowing Meade the reins to the Army of the Potomac. For Meade's part, he bristled under Grant's proximity, especially after having to defend his performance at the battle of Gettysburg to the congressional Joint Committee on the Conduct of the War in the winter of 1863-64. It was bad enough to have had to answer allegations from old foes like Daniel Sickles and Dan Butterfield, but now to have his command and control of the army all but neutered by Grant's arrival was too much. Meade's chief of staff, Andrew Humphreys, summarized it neatly by writing later, "Such a mixed command was not calculated to produce the best result that either singly was capable of bringing about. It naturally caused some vagueness and uncertainty as to the exact sphere of each, and—sometimes took away from the positiveness, fulness [*sic*], and earnestness of the consideration of an intended operation or tactical movement that, had there been but one commander, would have had the most earnest attention and corresponding action."

The idea of the separation of command collapsed into a million pieces with Griffin's outburst. Grant, used to his almost-perfect coupling with William T. Sherman, saw Griffin's insubordination as an affront to command; Meade responded by reminding Grant, quite literally, that the latter did not know what he was talking about. Grant resumed his whittling and smoking cigars on the afternoon of May 5, but also began to take a more-directed involvement in the Army of the Potomac's movements—increasingly frustrating Meade as the campaign unfolded.

Charles Griffin's temper-fueled outburst served as a microcosm of the cracks in Grant's and Meade's intended plan for command of the army, but those cracks were not just limited to the army commanders. As John Rawlins's disgust attests, Grant's entire staff was far from impressed by the attitude of lower-echelon commanders in the Army of the Potomac, while Meade's staff, including Theodore Lyman, was ardently loyal to him. It bears noting that in Lyman's diary entry for May 5 nothing is mentioned of Meade buttoning up Grant's jacket—those details do not come until an 1880 speech Lyman delivered. By depicting Grant as a "little boy"— an infant—Lyman not-so-subtly postured his former commander over Grant: the wise and experienced Meade putting Grant into his place and guiding him through battle. In 1880, this was far from the narrative of the Grant who ultimately defeated Lee, paving the way to the White House, whereas Meade died in 1872, his services largely forgotten.

All of that lay in the future. For the present, Grant was, for all intents and purposes, culture-shocked by the Army of the Potomac's battlefield operations. As the campaign unfolded, he would not just need to learn his opponent, Robert E. Lee and the Army of Northern Virginia, but also his subordinates, Meade and the Army of the Potomac.

Ryan Quint lives in Virginia and works for the National Park Service. He is the author of Determined to Stand and Fight: The Battle of Monocacy, July 9, 1864.

Grant's presence with the Army of the Potomac proved an awkward command structure as the Overland Campaign progressed, and while Meade chafed under it, he never publicly protested. Quoting a newspaper account, he described it as "'the Army of the Potomac, directed by Grant, commanded by Meade, and led by Hancock, Sedgwick and Warren,' which is quite a good distinction, and about hits the nail on the head."

While he complained privately that Grant's star continually eclipsed his own, he also showed genuine respect and admiration for Grant, whom he called "a good soldier, of great force of character, honest and upright, of pure purposes. . . . [H]e is, in my judgment, the best man the war has yet produced."

Grant, for his part, expressed nothing but satisfaction for Meade, and on May 13, he recommended Meade for promotion to major general in the regular army (Meade had been a major general of volunteers). "General Meade has more than met my most sanguine expectations," Grant wrote, calling Meade one of "the fittest officers for large commands I have come in contact with."

Where's Burnside?

APPENDIX C
BY CHRIS MACKOWSKI

Today, Maj. Gen. Ambrose P. Burnside is best known for his extravagant facial hair. In 1864, the affable Burnside was best known among his peers for his "genius for slowness."

Burnside had once commanded the Army of the Potomac, but after the debacle at Fredericksburg, Virginia, in December of 1862, followed by the disastrous "Mud March" the following January, Burnside resigned. The whiskered general assumed command of his old Ninth Corps, and together they shuffled from assignment to assignment—including a contest against James Longstreet's detached corps at Knoxville, Tennessee, in November of 1863.

When Grant assumed command of all Union armies, he recalled the Ninth Corps from Tennessee. Because Burnside outranked Maj. Gen. George Gordon Meade, commander of the Army of the Potomac, Grant could not incorporate the Ninth Corps into the army without ruffling feathers. Nonetheless, Grant moved the Ninth Corps in concert with the Army of the Potomac, issuing orders to Burnside that worked in tandem with the orders Grant issued Meade.

Things went wrong almost from the beginning.

On May 4, the Ninth Corps brought up the rear of the advancing Federal column. On May 5, when battle erupted, Grant ordered Burnside to support Warren along the Orange Turnpike. Burnside never made it into position even though his corps was only a short march away. After the war, Grant tried to put a positive face on it, noting some of Burnside's troops had "marched a distance of over 30 miles, crossing both the Rappahannock and Rapidan Rivers. Considering that a large proportion (probably two-thirds) of his command was composed of new troops, unaccustomed to marches and carrying the accouterments of a soldier, this was a remarkable march."

On the night of May 5, Burnside met with Meade and the Army of the Potomac's corps commanders. When ordered to break camp at 2:00 a.m. the following morning, Burnside happily assured everyone they could count on his troops to be ready to break camp "by half past two!"—apparently oblivious to the half-hour delay he'd enthusiastically built into the schedule.

Burnside made his headquarters for a time at the Wilderness Tavern. All that remains today are the ruins of one of the outbuildings. The site is accessible from the eastbound lane of Route 3 or by the Wilderness Run walking path from Ellwood. (cm)

After the war, Burnside's career once more revived. He served as the first president of the National Rifle Association and was thrice elected to the governorship of Rhode Island. He also represented Rhode Island in the United States Senate. Burnside died on September 13, 1881. (fsnmp)

Burnside's coordinated advance that next morning, on May 6, made up a crucial component of the assault Grant had ordered for 4:30 a.m. However, Hancock had to push his attack along the Plank Road on his own because Burnside failed to show at the appointed hour. "I knew it!" Hancock exclaimed. "Just what I expected." Burnside, it turned out, had stopped for breakfast.

"No one had expected much from Burnside," says historian Gordon Rhea, "and his failure to meet Grant's timetable was viewed as but another example of his inveterate slowness."

The Wilderness itself foiled Burnside even further. "The difficulty of making a way through the dense forests prevented Burnside from getting up in time to be of any service on the forenoon of the sixth," Grant later recalled, gracious in his understatement.

As the Overland Campaign unfolded, Burnside's corps would prove the Federals's weak link. "The inferiority of the 9th Corps begins now to show a good deal," one of Meade's staff officers complained, singling

Affable Burnside spends some time reading the paper and talking over the day's events with photographer Matthew Brady. (loc)

out the corps's "straggling and the general comparative want of tone and discipline." They would be stymied on several occasions at Spotsylvania Court House, and on May 24, they would be given the unenviable—and unachievable—task of attacking the Gibraltar of the Confederate line at North Anna.

Burnside would meet his eventual ruin on July 30, 1864, when a planned assault against the Confederate line at Petersburg would end in one of the most infamous disasters of the war: the battle of the Crater. Because of his mismanagement of events, Burnside was reassigned, where he waited out the remainder of the war in limbo— an ignoble ending for a man who, according to Burnside biographer William Marvel, had the "unqualified faith" of his men after capturing the North Carolina coast in 1862. "To them he was invincible," Marvel wrote; "wherever Ambrose Burnside went, victory should soon follow."

Members of the United States Colored Troops served with the IX Corps during the Overland Campaign, marking the first appearance of black soldiers in the Eastern Theater. "They were fine looking men, and were anxious to have a 'hand in' as soon as possible," one observer noted. While the black soldiers did not take part in the fighting at the Wilderness, they played a valuable role behind the scenes—and they anxiously waited for their opportunity to get into the fight (as they do here, in the lines outside Petersburg). As Grant's Overland Campaign continued, their time on the front lines would come. (phcw)

Unfriendly Fire
The Wounding of James Longstreet

APPENDIX D
BY CHRIS MACKOWSKI &
KRISTOPHER D. WHITE

The story of James Longstreet's wounding in the Wilderness is frequently eclipsed by a similar incident a year earlier: the accidental wounding of Thomas Jonathan "Stonewall" Jackson during the battle of Chancellorsville.

One year and four days prior to Longstreet's wounding, on May 2, 1863, less than four miles away, Jackson sustained mortal injuries when his men accidentally opened fire on him as he engaged in a nighttime reconnaissance.

While the specific circumstances differed, there were still many parallels. Both men were lieutenant generals. Both had overseen highly successful flanking maneuvers around a superior Union foe.

Also like Jackson, Longstreet was looking to follow up on his victory and keep momentum rolling. Longstreet and his staff rode forward at the head of a fresh brigade, the men "dressed in new uniforms made of cloth so dark a gray as to be almost black," said one Confederate. Their brigade commander, Brig. Gen. Micah Jenkins, "his face flushed with joy" at the Confederate success thus far, urged his men to cheer "lustily" for Longstreet.

Meanwhile, elements of Longstreet's flank attack still groped through the tangled forest and confusion. The 12th Virginia, which had been holding the right flank of Brig. Gen. William Mahone's brigade, got separated from the regiment next to it. The men of the 12th had to veer around one of the forest fires burning in the Wilderness, and then, following the contour of the ground, found themselves advancing along the bottom of a dip between two pieces of high ground.

Hidden from view as they were by the gully they occupied, the 12th Virginia neither saw their fellow Confederates to the left nor were they seen by the reforming Federals just 100 yards or so to their right. Ahead of them, though, across the Plank Road, they could see scattered remnants of other Federal units, and they crossed the road to do battle. Realizing they were the only unit across the road, though, the Virginians quickly "wheeled around so as to be parallel with the road," said James E. Philips, who was in the regiment. This

On the north side of the Orange Plank Road, the ground drops off steeply. Some of Longstreet's men, lost in the woods, approached the road from this low ground. This is roughly the perspective those men had as Longstreet's party appeared on the road (as depicted in the sketch on the following page). (cm)

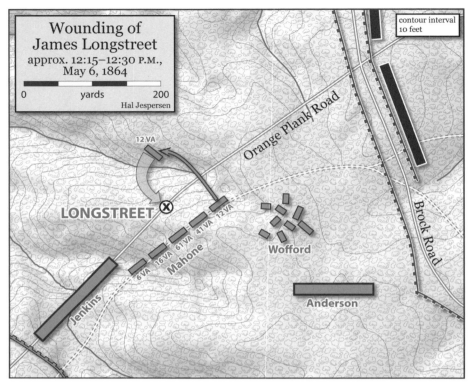

WOUNDING OF JAMES LONGSTREET—As Federals fell back to the Brock Road to regroup, the remnants of the men from Moxley Sorrel's flank attack continued to sweep through the forest. Anderson's brigade and Wofford's—the most discombobulated of the Confederate units—tried to regroup. Mahone's pushed onward. The 12th Virginia, veering around a forest fire, followed fleeing Federals across the Plank Road, then got themselves turned around. Into the confusion rode Longstreet, intending to lead Jenkins's brigade into the melee as fresh reinforcements.

would bring the 12th Virginia up out of the low ground, advancing back toward the road up the northern slope of one of the hillocks they'd been skirting.

Longstreet and the cheering column of dark-garbed soldiers traveled east on the Orange Plank Road just as the 12th Virginia approached the road through the woods on the road's north side. Those men, "some distance off in the thick underbrush, hearing the cheers and seeing this body of dark-uniformed men, took them for Yankees and fired a volley," said a Confederate officer.

The rest of Mahone's brigade, meanwhile, had stopped to dress ranks and reform. They were lined up between 35 and 75 yards to the south of the Plank Road. In the absence of the 12th Virginia, the 41st Virginia now held the brigade's right flank. When the 12th VA opened fire, they thought the gunfire was directed at them, so they returned fire.

"In the shaded light of the dense tangle, a shot or

two went off, then more, and finally a strong fusillade," said Sorrel, who was riding next to Longstreet.

"Steady, men! For God's sake, steady!" yelled Jenkins just before he slumped in his saddle with a bullet wound to the head.

At the same moment, Longstreet "received a severe shock from a minie ball passing through my throat and right shoulder," the general recalled. A newspaper account published on May 28 provided more specifics: "The ball struck him on the right of the larynx, passing under the skin, carrying away a part of the spine of the scapula, and coming out behind the right shoulder."

Sorrel, who'd been looking at Longstreet at that moment, saw the bullet hit. "He was a heavy man, with a very firm seat in the saddle, but he was actually lifted straight up and came down hard," the chief of staff said.

Longstreet settled back in his seat and started to ride on, "waving his left hand . . . to Mahone's troops, who

The 12th Virginia had crossed the road while "hunting Yankees" and so were looking for a fight when Longstreet's party appeared. (fsnmp)

"None but seasoned soldiers like the First Corps could have done even that much," bragged Longstreet's aide, Moxley Sorrel, recalling he First Corps's arrival on the battlefield on May 6. "I have always thought that in its entire splendid history the simple act of forming line in that dense undergrowth, under heavy fire and with the Third Corps men pushing to the rear through the ranks, was perhaps its greatest performance for steadiness and inflexible courage and discipline." (fsnmp)

recognized him and stopped, horror-stricken at what they had done," Hawkins said. But Longstreet quickly realized the severity of his wound. "[T]he flow of blood admonished me that my work for the day was done," the general said.

The leading files of Jenkins brigade fell out of line and prepared to fire into the woods when another of Longstreet's commanders, Maj. Gen. Joseph Kershaw, who'd escaped injury, dashed his horse into their ranks. In a clear voice, he called "F-r-i-e-n-d-s!" The Virginians "instantaneously realized the position of things and fell on their faces where they stood," Kershaw said.

Longstreet, "who had stood there like a lion at bay," Dawson said, "reeled as the blood poured down over his breast, and was evidently badly hurt." Jenkins, insensible, convulsed on the ground as one of his best friends tried to comfort him. Two other staffers were also killed.

Confederates on both sides of the road looked on in horrified astonishment at what they'd done. At least one witness thought the casualty list could have been worse. "Fortunately they fired high, or there would have been a terrible slaughter," he said. "As it was . . . the effect was horrible."

One possible reason to account for the high fire was that the 12th Virginia had just crested the fairly steep hill on the north side of the road. Firing slightly uphill would have made their shots go high.

As Longstreet turned to ride back, he swooned. His staff immediately dismounted him and laid him near the foot of a tree. "He was almost choked with blood," Sorrel noted.

"It seemed that he had not many minutes to live," Dawson recalled. In "desperate haste," he rode off to the nearest field hospital and found Dr. John Syng Dorsey Cullen, the First Corps's medical director. "I made him jump on my horse, and bade him, for Heaven's sake, ride as rapidly as he could to the front where Longstreet was," Dawson said.

Longstreet, meanwhile, with bloody foam bubbling from his lips, beckoned members of the staff to lean close. In a whisper, he urged someone to find General Lee and "tell him that the enemy were in utter rout, and if pressed, would all be his before night," Haskell said.

Cullen soon arrived and staunched the bleeding, and Longstreet was quickly loaded on a litter into an ambulance. Kershaw urged speed. Federal artillerist, who'd heard the exchange of gunfire, had begun to lob shells in their direction. "Fortunately, the shots were passing high but were nevertheless dangerous," an observer said.

Jenkins, who also received medical attention, did not

fare as well. He babbled incoherently, gray matter oozing from the wound in his forehead. His boyhood friend, Col. Ashbury Coward knelt down to comfort him. The downed brigadier would last a few hours before finally dying.

The initial prognosis for Longstreet looked dire. His staff soon placed him into an ambulance and moved him to a field hospital in the rear, near Parker's Store. "The members of his staff surrounded the vehicle, some riding in front, some on one side and some on the other, and some behind," said Artillerist Robert Styles, who encountered the group on their trek. "I never on any occasion during the four years of the war saw a group of officers and gentlemen more deeply distressed. They were literally bowed down with grief. All of them were in tears."

When Stiles rode up to the ambulance and looked in, he noticed that Cullen had removed Longstreet's hat, coat, and boots. "The blood had paled out of his face and its somewhat gross aspect was gone. I noticed how white and dome-like his great forehead looked," Stiles recalled.

He also noted the fine gauze undervest Longstreet wore, stained with the black-red gore from his breast and shoulder. "Longstreet very quietly moved his unwounded arm," Stiles said, "and, with his thumb and two fingers, carefully lifted the saturated undershirt from his chest, holding it up a moment, and heaved a deep sign. He is not dead, I said to myself, and his is calm and entirely master of the situation."

Soldiers lining the road, who could not see Longstreet, began to say the general was dead and that they were only being told he was wounded to hide the calamity from them. "Hearing this repeated from time to time," Longstreet later wrote, "I raised my hat with my left hand, when the burst of voices and the flying of hats in the air eased my pains somewhat."

Not long thereafter, the ambulance met Lee. "I shall not soon forget the sadness in his face, and the almost despairing movement of his hands, when he was told Longstreet had fallen," Dawson remembered.

"A blunder!" wrote Lee's aid, Walter Taylor. "Call it so; the old deacon [Jackson] would say that God willed it thus."

Comparisons to Jackson's ill fate proved inevitable. "By some strange fatality the flank movement, patterned after Jackson's of the year before in the same vicinity, had had the same brilliant success in routing the enemy in a panic, & the same melancholy termination . . ." wrote a Confederate officer.

"Heaven grant that Lee may not lose his left arm now, as he lost his right arm then!" wrote a newspaper correspondent.

A successful civil engineer prior to the war, William "Little Billy" Mahone had worked on several major railroad construction projects prior to the war, including a rail line to connect Fredericksburg and Orange. Although the project was never finished, Mahone had opportunity to take advantage of his work in an unexpected way. In order to get his men into position for their flank attack on May 6, Mahone led them down the unfinished railroad cut and, in its shelter, formed them into line of battle. (fsnmp)

Just to the northeast of the tour stop for Longstreet's wounding, the road dips into a swale before rising up to the Brock Road/Plank Road intersection. The dip explains why the 12th Virginia had been able to cross the open road so close to the Federal line without anyone seeing them. Anyone approaching from the southwest, from the direction Longstreet rode, would not have been able to see the Virginians cross, either. (cm)

"It seems almost impossible to prevent blunders of this kind during the excitement and confusion of a battle in such a place where . . . the contending forces are fighting unseen foes even when at short range and almost face to face," said a Confederate cavalryman. One participant, trying to explain the flare-up of gunfire, feared "that we had ridden into the midst of the enemy, and that nothing remained but to sell our lives dearly."

Longstreet, for his part, called the incident "an honest mistake, one of the accidents of the war."

Longstreet was bundled off to Lynchburg to recover. "He is very feeble and nervous and suffers much from his wound," observed one of the women who tended him on a stopover in Charlottesville. "He sheds tears on the slightest provocation and apologizes for it. He says he does not see why a bullet going through a man's shoulder should make a baby of him."

Once in Lynchburg, he stayed for a time with a relative, but Federal raiding parties made the area unsafe, so Longstreet was moved even farther south—to Augusta, Georgia. While recuperating there, Longstreet received a letter from Lee asking him to not get captured by William T. Sherman.

Lee's Old Warhorse would not return to the army until October. Never again would he regain the use of his right arm, and his once-powerful voice would never again rise much above a whisper.

In his memoirs, Ulysses Grant acknowledged that Longstreet's wounding had an impact on the battle. "His loss was a severe one to Lee," Grant wrote, "and compensated in a great measure for the mishap, or misapprehensions, which had fallen to our lot during the day."

While Longstreet's wounding had an immediate impact on the battle—"Longstreet's fall seemed actually to paralyse our whole corps," wrote artillery chief E. Porter Alexander—Lee would come to understand the real ramifications of the accident in the weeks to come. With Longstreet gone, Lee faced a leadership crisis in his army. Inexperience, illness, and death plagued the Army of Northern Virginia at the corps level, and in Longstreet's absence, Lee had no one to fill the void. Also, as the war took a decidedly defensive turn for Lee, the commander missed the counsel of his most defensive-minded general. Longstreet was the only high-ranking officer in Lee's army who personally knew Ulysses S. Grant and so would have been able to offer any insight about the Federal commander—something Lee sorely lacked.

"[T]he evil genius of the South is still hovering over those desolate woods," a Confederate wrote, evoking the accidents that wounded both Jackson and Longstreet. "We almost seem to be struggling against destiny itself."

Despite a bullet in the brain, Micah Jenkins didn't die immediately. In his fading delirium, he cheered his troops, not actually conscious of what he was doing or where they were. (fsnmp)

KRISTOPHER D. WHITE, *a co-founder of Emerging Civil War, is senior education manager at the American Battlefield Trust and author of numerous books and articles.*

The Wilderness as Wilderness, Then and Now

APPENDIX E
BY GREGG KNEIPP

In the 1860s, the Wilderness battlefield was a recovering forest. It had been cut over multiple times for the iron furnaces in the area, where the wood was turned into charcoal and used for smelting the iron out of the iron ore found in the vicinity. When a forest is cut over or clear-cut, it starts out in the beginning stages of forest regrowth, also known as the restart of forest succession.

When a forest is cut over, grasses and herbivorous plants such as milkweed and goldenrod fill in the open spaces. Virginia red cedars come in soon after, along with Virginia pines. Tulip poplars and sweetgums are the first hardwoods to grow in the open areas. Hardwoods are trees like oak, hickory, and maple and are usually deciduous, meaning their leaves fall off seasonally; their wood is generally harder than conifers (pine trees).

Since mature hardwood trees were cut down to create the fuel for the iron furnaces, the stumps of these trees would send out sprouts almost immediately—within the first growing season. These new growth suckers, coming from the mature root stock of the adult trees that were cut down, have all the food reserves from the root stock, so all their energy directly goes into the growth of the new stalks. Tremendous growth occurs—10 or more feet in 10 years. The quick growth results in thick forests.

Virginia pines, also quick to start in the open areas, can grow just as fast, so there can be a new, thick, shrubby forest within a 10-year period.

After a number of years of undisturbed growth, the hardwoods dominate these new forests. The herbaceous layers that were composed of grasses and plants like boneset, black-eyed Susan, and pokeberry die out because of the competition for sunlight, which the hardwoods will eventually win. The shade from these new forests kills the pine and cedar seedlings, too, and eventually causes their overall demise. Only the hardiest and tallest of the hardwoods will survive and recreate the forest that once existed before the clear-cut—and which now exists again in the Wilderness—one of mature oaks, hickories, and maples.

Some patches of tall Virginia pines will not

Milkweed offers excellent habitat for butterflies in the summer before wisping away in the fall. (cm)

Fungi of all shapes and sizes take advantage of the ecological diversity in the Wilderness, from damp, decaying leafbeds (left) to open, full-sun lawns (right). (cm)(cm)

endure, as the Virginia pine seedlings need too much sunlight and will eventually die out. When the mature Virginia pines die and fall down over time, shade-tolerant hardwoods—trees that will eventually create the canopy of a mature hardwood forest—will replace them. Smaller, sub-canopy trees will survive in the mature hardwood forest, depending on soil type, moisture availability, and topography—plants such as American holly, American dogwood, and blackgum, among others.

If and when another major disturbance occurs, such as a hurricane or tornado blowdown, the whole cycle will start over in the area of disturbance, similar to the area bounded by Hooker Drive and Ely's Ford Road in Chancellorsville. The Chancellorsville History Trail on the Chancellorsville Battlefield shows a great example of what the Wilderness would have looked like. To see this thicket forest, start at the Bullock house site on Bullock Road. On foot, cross over Ely's Ford Road towards Hooker Drive, and follow the trail. Within one tenth of a mile, you will be walking in an area of blowdown from Hurricane Isabel from September 2003 that resembles the Wilderness of the 1860's.

When the forest was clear-cut for the iron works, deer were probably not very abundant. Deer thrive on areas of habitat with large amounts of underbrush or shrubby thickets where there is plenty to eat, as they usually browse on the new, tender vegetation and the buds of shrubs; they will also graze on grass, if available. The shrubby forests also provide lots of cover from predators (animals that eat other animals) and human hunters. In the open forest, there is not as much to eat, and the area is wide open, so the deer are easily seen and easy prey to predators and humans. The newer shrubby forests, though, would have given the few remaining deer a respite and allowed them to recover somewhat from the relentless and unregulated hunting in the early to mid-1800s.

Today, there is an overabundance of deer in the area; there are not many hunters, and almost no natural predators to keep the deer numbers in balance with their food sources. The park's neighbors see the results of the large number of deer in the area because the deer like to eat their gardens and ornamental plantings. However, in the last 10 to 20 years, coyotes have migrated into the area from the north and west and have become the only real predator of deer on the east coast. These new predators are helping control the number of deer and reducing their impact on the vegetation of the local forests.

Deer are overabundant in the park. (cm)

Smaller animals, like the Virginia opossum, raccoons, rabbits, and foxes also prefer the thicker, shrubby forests for the same reasons deer do: forests provide thick cover for protection from predators and more food to eat for those animals that eat vegetation (herbivores), like rabbits.

Many songbirds prefer this thick cover as well for nesting; however, there are other songbirds that prefer open fields as well as those that prefer mature forests. Songbirds are specialists when it comes to habitat (areas where they choose to live). Birds like the northern flicker, veery, scarlet tanager, and the pileated woodpecker are much more common in mature forests, but back in the 1860s, there would have been many more chipping sparrows, blue birds, eastern meadowlarks, and yellow-throated vireo in the shrubby thickets.

Looking even smaller—at salamanders, snakes, turtles, and frogs—different habitat types come into play. For amphibians—salamanders, frogs, and toads—wetlands are more important factors in their habitat selection, as these small animals need dependable water bodies to complete their life cycles. The amphibians need

GREGG KNEIPP, *the Natural Resources Manager at Fredericksburg and Spotsylvania National Military Park, has worked for the National Park Service for almost 26 years and at his current park for the last 16 years. He holds a B.S. in Wildlife and Fisheries Management from Frostburg State University and an M.S. in Environmental Sciences from Johns Hopkins University.*

to lay their eggs in water bodies that will not be likely to dry out so they can hatch and metamorphose. Frogs, who need a fairly constant source of water year round, cannot stray far from water, but salamanders and toads, which can get by with less water throughout the year,

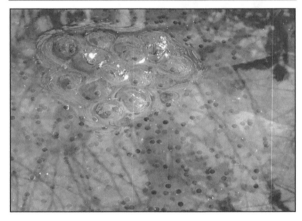

Streams and small pools (top) provide vital habitat for amphibians, turtles, fish, and a host of invertebrates. Even some earthworks that collect spring rains can provide seasonal habitat for frog eggs (bottom). (cm)(cm)

can move about without a constant water source so long as they have water to sustain their reproductive efforts.

Generally speaking, mature forested wetlands provide better and more stable sources of water for these animals because the wetlands are shaded and their temperatures are more constant. In contrast, wetlands in shrubby areas tend to have greater temperature swings and are more exposed to sunlight, and therefore more likely to dry out before these amphibians can complete their reproduction.

In addition, for salamanders, they are more likely to find shelter in mature forests, as salamanders like to hide under large, decaying logs; in the shrubby areas, they are unlikely to find the logs they like to live under.

Snakes and turtles are fairly independent when it comes to forests as compared to shrubby areas. The reptiles can usually be found equally throughout, as long as there is enough shade in the short, shrubby forests, allowing them to cool off during the summer. Both snakes and turtles are cold-blooded and take on the temperature of their environment, unlike the warm-blooded mammals (raccoons, rabbits, foxes, skunks, coyotes) that self-regulate their body temperature.

Another animal visitor to the open, shrubby forest are various butterflies and other insects attracted to milkweed, butterfly weed, and goldenrod—plants that require the plentiful sunlight of a less-dense canopy. They can be seen flitting among the wildflowers found in the

Wilderness's open areas. However, as the forest matures, these herbaceous plants are shaded and die out. These insects are less likely to be found in the mature forests.

Generally speaking, there is a large difference between the mature hardwood forests that constitute the Wilderness today, as compared to the thick, short, shrubby forests of the 1860s. The mature forests provide more constant temperatures, better quality wetlands, and better habitat for forest-loving animals, such as pileated woodpeckers, salamanders, and other woodland creatures. The shorter, thicker, brushy forests of the 1860s provided better habitat for wildlife that needed thick cover for protection from predators and provided better food sources for herbivores. Overall, different types of animals could be found in the different forests, with some overlap between the two types— some animals being found in both but preferring one over the other for food or cover.

Over time, the shrubby forests turned into mature forests, forcing some denizens to look for a home elsewhere, in some other disturbed area where the forest succession had started over from open field back into the mature forest. And, over time, the wetlands from the open, shrubby areas became a higher quality habitat for wildlife as the wetlands became more shaded and provided a more stable habitat to the amphibians that inhabit those wetlands.

Snakes and snails and. . . . That's what the Wilderness is made of. (cm)(cm)

The next time you walk a battlefield, consider not only the military history but its natural history, as well. In areas of increasing development like Spotsylvania County, protected forests like National Park Service property become important refuge for animals facing increasing pressure on their habitats.

Building a Battlefield:
The C.C.C. in the Wilderness

APPENDIX F
BY REBEKAH OAKES

At Fredericksburg and Spotsylvania National Military Park, a New Deal-era utility building now houses modern maintenance equipment. Stone letters denoting CCC camp MP-4 are obscured by the tall grass of the Wilderness battlefield's Saunders Field. Occasionally, a visitor or local resident finds an artifact belonging not to the Army of the Potomac or Army of Northern Virginia, but instead to Franklin Roosevelt's Tree Army. The Civilian Conservation Corps (CCC), including Wilderness Camp MP-4, left numerous intentional marks on America's Civil War battlefields. They left a few unintentional signs of their presence, as well. However, their story is one not often told.

Between 1933 and 1941, five companies of the CCC called the north side of Saunders Field home. Although most signs of their camp's presence have been obliterated in favor of a rehabilitated battlefield landscape and the modern Wilderness Exhibit Shelter, aerial photos from the 1930s show a very different scene. The camp included company barracks, an administrative building, a utility building, a mess hall, a recreation hall, and sanitation facilities. Hints of the camp, such as the stone letters, the utility building, and depressions in the landscape, remain today. However, more tangible reminders of the CCC's presence can be found in the work the men completed on the battlefields themselves.

Camp MP-4 engaged in a myriad of conservation work. Aside from planting trees, which the CCC as a whole is widely known for, enrollees in the Wilderness also cleared brush from roads, visitor areas, and earthworks. They graded park roads, constructed telephone lines, and cut foot trails. In addition to park development, the enrollees helped make the park safer by reducing fire hazards. "Landscaping and improving" was another significant duty of enrollees; this umbrella term included the now-controversial decision to fortify, or "build up," the existing battlefield earthworks to mimic their Civil War-era appearance. Trench sodding, as well as many other landscaping techniques, were conducted with the goal of giving the battlefield landscape a "rustic," or "natural," appearance. Other jobs included marking park boundaries, constructing fences and guardrails, and tree insect pest control. MP-4 enrollees worked on not only the Wilderness Battlefield, but on all of the battlefields

Hidden in the tall grass of Saunders Field behind the exhibit shelter, concrete letters left over from Civilian Conservation Corps camp MP-4 still mark what had once been the camp's front gate. (cm)

Once a cornfield, Saunders Field boasted a bumper crop of barracks in the 1930s. (fsnmp)

in the park, including such jobs as tree pruning in the National Cemetery.

Some enrollees at Camp MP-4 also acted as historic guides for visitors to the battlefields—a popular, free service visitors were encouraged to take advantage of through prominent signage. The guides were an integral part of the visitor services offered by the park in the late 1930s. As an example, between July 1, 1937, and February 28, 1938, camp enrollees had put in 821 "man days" as educational guides. However, this practice also reflected the segregated nature of both the CCC and the early administration of Fredericksburg & Spotsylvania. Only white enrollees were given the opportunity to serve as historic guides; the one company of African American enrollees to reside at Saunders Field was not afforded the same occupation.

Just as important as the conservation of the landscape was the CCC's attempt at human conservation, or the rehabilitation and general betterment of the enrollees themselves. Camp reports frequently comment on the gained weight and overall increase in the boys's physical strength. Careful attention was paid to the daily menu, ensuring a balanced diet including one salad, one pint of milk, one vegetable, one fruit, and two meat or meat substitute dishes were served. Rules also dictated variety, forbidding the same dish or two dishes made from the same product from being served in one day.

Several sports were available to enrollees, including baseball, basketball, volleyball, track and field events, and boxing. Courses were offered in personal hygiene. Educational opportunities were another significant benefit of being enrolled in the CCC. At Camp MP-4, boys could take a variety of courses. They ranged from elementary classes such as Reading Class for Illiterates, to more advanced courses such as Civil Engineering and Physiology, to vocational subjects including Auto Mechanics and Accounting, and even music classes. Camp residents enjoyed a library collection of more than 90 books. The CCC was not only concerned with the enrollees's present betterment, but their future opportunities for employment, as well.

From the Orange Turnpike, the CCC Camp offered a neat and orderly appearance. (fsnmp)

Camp administrators also encouraged cultural and social education. Enrollees were able to visit town on Wednesday evenings and weekends, and "talking pictures," lecturers, and entertainers were regularly brought in. Fairly frequent trips were planned to sites throughout the area, including one to Washington, D.C. Highlights of the trip to the nation's capital

included the Washington and Lincoln memorials, the gallery of the House of Representatives, and the Smithsonian, where "some wanted to see the animals, some the aircraft," but all "looked over Lindy's 'Spirit of St. Louis' with many a thrill," one later reported. The boys enjoyed trips to Shenandoah National Park, dances with the local community, and even at one point cared for a 130-pound St. Bernard named Bowser. In addition to subscribing to several newspapers, including the CCC's national newspaper *Happy Days*, the camp produced its own periodical.

Robert Fechner, the national director of the CCC, visits with a group at the Chancellorsville Contact Station, which was manned by enrollees from the Wilderness camp. (fsnmp)

Of all the recreational opportunities afforded to enrollees at Camp MP-4, baseball was perhaps the most important. The camp's baseball team was able to enter a league with other camps in the area, and it became fairly competitive. Newspaper accounts describing the games are reminiscent of professional sports reporting,

Although records are incomplete, somewhere between 800 and 1,000 different enrollees were housed at the Wilderness CCC Camp between 1933 and 1941. (fsnmp)

such as one from July 7, 1934, which described "a game packed with thrills and streaked with comedy," in which the company won its third sub-district league victory over the "victim," Co. 1241 of Fort Hunt, Virginia. The score was an impressive 20 to 1. Baseball became so important to the camp's morale that one of the most documented incidents in the camp's history was the brief loss of access to the field where enrollees practiced. The owner of the land on the south side of Saunders Field, who had previously allowed enrollees to use his land for baseball practice free of charge, requested a payment of $10.00 per month in March of 1938. Although the owner of the land, James Dempsey, was friendly with the Camp Superintendent at the time, camp documentation reveals tension existed between Dempsey and Company Commander Leo Poindexter. This boiled over into a verbal confrontation, culminating when Poindexter ordered Dempsey off camp property. The incident was eventually resolved when the camp secured use of a field a mile farther down the road, and Capt. Poindexter was relocated. In a moment of irony, camp enrollees responded to a call for assistance with a building fire that same month and were able to save the structure. That building belonged to Mr. Dempsey.

As the baseball field incident illustrates, the eight years of the camp's existence was not without incident. In the first year of the camp's administration, 27 enrollees were dishonorably discharged, including 18 in one instance following a food strike in the mess hall. Many of the issues within the camp seemed to stem from clashes between camp administrators. In August of 1934, a camp resident wrote an anonymous letter complaining of trouble in the mess hall, meals "have been lousy and not enough," and contradictory orders given to enrollees. As the cause of this issue, he cited a power struggle between the camp's captain and the mess officer. Investigating officers largely brushed these concerns aside, but the captain was rapidly removed to another location. The incident over the baseball field in 1938 most likely stemmed from friction between the camp superintendent and the company commander.

REBEKAH OAKES (Becky) is a former staff historian at Fredericksburg and Spotsylvania National Military Park. She is fascinated by historical memory, battlefield landscapes, and the history of the National Park Service.

Overall, though, for a program that placed hundreds of boys in the midst of an unfamiliar community in a time of great social turmoil, the Wilderness CCC camp had a history fairly free of major conflict.

All that remains of the former camp is a building now used by the NPS as a maintenance shed. (cm)

The story of Wilderness Camp MP-4 is captivating, significant, and regularly overlooked. Although the first clash of Robert E. Lee and Ulysses S. Grant within the impenetrable thicket of the Wilderness is the story that attracts visitors to this battlefield, the work the Civilian Conservation Corps did here was fundamental to the development of the park itself. The CCC's presence here goes beyond a repurposed building and a footnote in park history. The story of these enrollees is part of a moment of turmoil that defined a nation, just as the Civil War did 75 years before, and of a nation's attempt to rebuild, to conserve. The camp's enrollees had experiences on these fields that changed and defined the rest of their lives. The work these boys did here, the education they received, and even the baseball they played, not only transformed the nation's cultural resources, but the lives of its people.

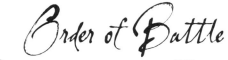

THE BATTLE OF THE WILDERNESS

ARMY OF THE UNITED STATES
Lt. Gen. Ulysses S. Grant

ARMY OF THE POTOMAC
Maj. Gen. George G. Meade

Provost Guard Brig. Gen. Marsena R. Patrick
1st Massachusetts Cavalry, Companies C and D • 80th New York Infantry (20th Militia)
3rd Pennsylvania Cavalry • 68th Pennsylvania Infantry • 114th Pennsylvania Infantry
Volunteer Engineer Brigade Brig. Gen. Henry W. Benham
50th New York Engineers
Battalion U.S. Engineers Capt. George H. Mendell
Guard and Orderlies *Independent Company Oneida (New York) Cavalry*

SECOND CORPS Maj. Gen. Winfield S. Hancock
ESCORT *1st Vermont Cavalry, Company M*
FIRST DIVISION Brig. Gen. Francis C. Barlow
First Brigade Col. Nelson A. Miles
26th Michigan • 61st New York • 81st Pennsylvania • 140th Pennsylvania • 183rd Pennsylvania

Second Brigade Col. Thomas A. Smyth
28th Massachusetts • 63rd New York • 69th New York • 88th New York • 116th Pennsylvania

Third Brigade Col. Paul Frank
39th New York • 52nd New York • 57th New York • 111th New York • 125th New York
126th New York

Fourth Brigade Col. John R. Brooke
2nd Delaware • 64th New York • 66th New York • 53rd Pennsylvania • 145th Pennsylvania
148th Pennsylvania

SECOND DIVISION Brig. Gen. John Gibbon
Provost Guard *2nd Company Minnesota Sharpshooters*
First Brigade Brig. Gen. Alexander S. Webb
19th Maine • 1st Company Andrew (Massachusetts) Sharpshooters • 15th Massachusetts
19th Massachusetts • 20th Massachusetts • 7th Michigan • 42nd New York
59th New York • 82nd New York (2nd Militia)

Second Brigade Brig. Gen. Joshua T. Owen
152nd New York • 69th Pennsylvania • 71st Pennsylvania • 72nd Pennsylvania
106th Pennsylvania

Third Brigade Col. Samuel S. Carroll
14th Connecticut • 1st Delaware • 14th Indiana • 12th New Jersey • 10th New York Battalion
108th New York • 4th Ohio • 8th Ohio • 7th West Virginia

THIRD DIVISION Maj. Gen. David B. Birney
First Brigade Brig. Gen. J. H. Hobart Ward
20th Indiana • 3rd Maine • 40th New York • 86th New York • 124th New York
99th Pennsylvania • 110th Pennsylvania • 141st Pennsylvania • 2nd U.S. Sharpshooters

Second Brigade Brig. Gen. Alexander Hays
4th Maine • 17th Maine • 3rd Michigan • 5th Michigan • 93rd New York
57th Pennsylvania • 63rd Pennsylvania • 105th Pennsylvania • 1st U.S. Sharpshooters

FOURTH DIVISION Brig. Gen. Gershom Mott
First Brigade Col. Robert McAllister
1st Massachusetts • 16th Massachusetts • 5th New Jersey • 6th New Jersey • 7th New Jersey
8th New Jersey • 11th New Jersey • 26th Pennsylvania • 115th Pennsylvania

Second Brigade Col. William R. Brewster
11th Massachusetts • 70th New York • 71st New York • 72nd New York • 73rd New York
74th New York • 120th New York • 84th Pennsylvania

Artillery Brigade Col. John C. Tidball
6th Maine, Battery F • 10th Massachusetts, Battery • 1st New Hampshire, Battery
1st New York Light, Battery G • 4th New York Heavy, 3rd Battalion • 1st Pennsylvania, Battery F
1st Rhode Island, Battery A • 1st Rhode Island, Battery B • 4th United States, Battery K
5th United States, Batteries C and I

FIFTH CORPS Maj. Gen. Gouverneur K. Warren
Provost Guard *12th New York Battalion*
FIRST DIVISION Brig. Gen. Charles Griffin
First Brigade Brig. Gen. Romeyn B. Ayres
140th New York • 146th New York • 91st Pennsylvania • 155th Pennsylvania
2nd United States, Companies B, C, F, H, I, and K • 11th United States, Companies B, C, D, E,
F, and G, 1st Battalion • 12th United States, Companies A, B, C, D, and G, 1st Battalion
12th United States, Companies A, C, D, F, and H, 2nd Battalion • 14th United States, 1st Battalion
17th United States, Companies A, C, D, G, and H, 1st Battalion
17th United States, Companies A, B, and C, 2nd Battalion

Second Brigade Col. Jacob B. Sweitzer
9th Massachusetts • 22nd Massachusetts • 32nd Massachusetts • 4th Michigan
62nd Pennsylvania

Third Brigade Brig. Gen. Joseph J. Bartlett
20th Maine • 18th Massachusetts • 1st Michigan • 16th Michigan • 44th New York
83rd Pennsylvania • 118th Pennsylvania

SECOND DIVISION Brig. Gen. John C. Robinson
First Brigade Col. Samuel H. Leonard
16th Maine • 13th Massachusetts • 39th Massachusetts • 104th New York

Second Brigade Brig. Gen. Henry Baxter
*12th Massachusetts • 83rd New York (9th Militia) • 97th New York • 11th Pennsylvania
88th Pennsylvania • 90th Pennsylvania*

Third Brigade Col. Andrew W. Denison
1st Maryland • 4th Maryland • 7th Maryland • 8th Maryland

THIRD DIVISION Brig. Gen. Samuel W. Crawford
First Brigade Col. William McCandless
*1st Pennsylvania Reserves • 2nd Pennsylvania Reserves • 6th Pennsylvania Reserves
7th Pennsylvania Reserves • 11th Pennsylvania Reserves • 13th Pennsylvania Reserves (1st Rifles)*

Third Brigade Col. Joseph W. Fisher
*5th Pennsylvania Reserves • 8th Pennsylvania Reserves • 10th Pennsylvania Reserves
12th Pennsylvania Reserves*

FOURTH DIVISION Brig. Gen. James S. Wadsworth
First Brigade Brig. Gen. Lysander Cutler
*7th Indiana • 19th Indiana • 24th Michigan • 1st New York Battalion Sharpshooters
2nd Wisconsin • 6th Wisconsin • 7th Wisconsin*

Second Brigade Brig. Gen. James C. Rice
*76th New York • 84th New York (14th Militia) • 95th New York • 147th New York
56th Pennsylvania*

Third Brigade Col. Roy Stone
*121st Pennsylvania • 142nd Pennsylvania • 143rd Pennsylvania • 149th Pennsylvania
150th Pennsylvania*

Artillery Brigade Col. Charles S. Wainwright
*Massachusetts Light, Battery C • Massachusetts Light, Battery E • 1st New York, Battery D
1st New York, Batteries E and L • 1st New York, Battery H • 4th New York Heav., 2nd Battalion
1st Pennsylvania Light, Battery B • 4th United States, Battery B • 5th United States, Battery D*

SIXTH CORPS Maj. Gen. John Sedgwick
Escort *8th Pennsylvania Cavalry, Company A*
FIRST DIVISION Brig. Gen. Horatio G. Wright
First Brigade Col. Henry W. Brown
*1st New Jersey • 2nd New Jersey • 3rd New Jersey • 4th New Jersey • 10th New Jersey
15th New Jersey*

Second Brigade Col. Emory Upton
5th Maine • 121st New York • 95th Pennsylvania • 96th Pennsylvania

Third Brigade Brig. Gen. David A. Russell
6th Maine • 49th Pennsylvania • 119th Pennsylvania • 5th Wisconsin

Fourth Brigade Brig. Gen. Alexander Shaler
65th New York • 67th New York • 122nd New York • 82nd Pennsylvania (detachment)

SECOND DIVISION Brig. Gen. George W. Getty
First Brigade Brig. Gen. Frank Wheaton
*62nd New York • 93rd Pennsylvania • 98th Pennsylvania • 102nd Pennsylvania
139th Pennsylvania*

Second Brigade Col. Lewis A. Grant
2nd Vermont • 3rd Vermont • 4th Vermont • 5th Vermont • 6th Vermont

Third Brigade Brig. Gen. Thomas H. Neill
7th Maine • 43rd New York • 49th New York • 77th New York • 61st Pennsylvania

Fourth Brigade Brig. Gen. Henry L. Eustis
7th Massachusetts • 10th Massachusetts • 37th Massachusetts • 2nd Rhode Island

THIRD DIVISION Brig. Gen. James B. Ricketts
First Brigade Brig. Gen. William H. Morris
14th New Jersey • 106th New York • 151st New York • 87th Pennsylvania • 10th Vermont

Second Brigade Brig. Gen. Truman Seymour
*6th Maryland • 110th Ohio • 122nd Ohio • 126th Ohio • 67th Pennsylvania (detachment)
138th Pennsylvania*

Artillery Brigade Col. Charles H. Thompkins
*4th Maine, Battery D • 1st Massachusetts, Battery A • 1st New York Independent Battery
3rd New York Independent Battery • 4th New York Heavy, 1st Battalion
1st Rhode Island, Battery C • 1st Rhode Island, Battery E • 1st Rhode Island, Battery G
5th United States, Battery M*

CAVALRY CORPS Maj. Gen. Philip H. Sheridan
Escort *6th United States*
FIRST DIVISION Brig. Gen. Alfred A. Torbert
First Brigade Brig. Gen. George A. Custer
1st Michigan • 5th Michigan • 6th Michigan • 7th Michigan

Second Brigade Col. Thomas C. Devin
4th New York • 6th New York • 9th New York • 17th Pennsylvania

Reserve Brigade Brig. Gen. Wesley Merritt
*19th New York (1st Dragoons) • 6th Pennsylvania • 1st United States • 2nd United States
5th United States*

SECOND DIVISION Brig. Gen. David McM. Gregg
First Brigade Brig. Gen. Henry E. Davies, Jr.
1st Massachusetts • 1st New Jersey • 6th Ohio • 1st Pennsylvania

Second Brigade Col. J. Irvin Gregg
*1st Maine • 10th New York • 2nd Pennsylvania • 4th Pennsylvania • 8th Pennsylvania
16th Pennsylvania*

THIRD DIVISION Brig. Gen. James H. Wilson
Escort *8th Illinois (detachment)*
First Brigade Col. John B. McIntosh
1st Connecticut • 2nd New York • 5th New York • 18th Pennsylvania

Second Brigade Col. George H. Chapman
3nd Indiana • 8th New York • 1st Vermont

ARTILLERY Brig. Gen. Henry J. Hunt
ARTILLERY RESERVE Col. Henry S. Burton
First Brigade Col. J. Howard Kitching
6th New York Heavy • 15th New York Heavy

Second Brigade Maj. John A. Tompkins
*5th Maine, Battery E • 1st New Jersey, Battery A • 1st New Jersey, Battery B
5th New York Battery • 12th New York Battery • 1st New York, Battery B*

Third Brigade Maj. Robert H. Fitzhugh
*9th Massachusetts Battery • 15th New York Light • 1st New York, Battery C
11th New York Battery • 1st Ohio, Battery H • 5th United States, Battery E*

HORSE ARTILLERY
First Brigade Capt. James M. Robertson
*6th New York Battery • 2nd United States, Batteries B and L • 2nd United States, Battery D
2nd United States, Battery M • 4th United States, Battery A • 4th United States, Batteries C and E*

Second Brigade Capt. Dunbar R. Ransom
*1st United States, Batteries E and G • 1st United States, Batteries H and I • 1st United States,
Battery K • 2nd United States, Battery A • 2nd United States, Battery G • 3rd United States,
Batteries C, F, and K*

NINTH ARMY CORPS
Maj. Gen. Ambrose E. Burnside
(independent command not part of the Army of the Potomac)

Provost Guard *8th U.S. Infantry*
FIRST DIVISION Brig. Gen. Thomas G. Stevenson
First Brigade Col. Sumner Carruth
*35th Massachusetts • 56th Massachusetts • 57th Massachusetts • 59th Massachusetts
4th United States • 10th United States*

Second Brigade Col. Daniel Leasure
3rd Maryland • 21st Massachusetts • 100th Pennsylvania

Artillery
2nd Maine, Battery B • 14th Massachusetts Battery

SECOND DIVISION Brig. Gen. Robert B. Potter
First Brigade Col. Zenas R. Bliss
36th Massachusetts • 58th Massachusetts • 51st New York • 45th Pennsylvania
48th Pennsylvania • 7th Rhode Island

Second Brigade Col. Simon G. Griffin
31st Maine • 32nd Maine • 6th New Hampshire • 9th New Hampshire
11th New Hampshire • 17th Vermont

Artillery
11th Massachusetts Battery • 19th New York Battery

THIRD DIVISION Brig. Gen. Orlando B. Willcox
First Brigade Col. John F. Hartranft
2nd Michigan • 8th Michigan • 17th Michigan • 27th Michigan • 109th New York
51st Pennsylvania

Second Brigade Col. Benjamin C. Christ
1st Michigan Sharpshooters • 20th Michigan • 70th New York • 60th Ohio
50th Pennsylvania

Artillery
7th Maine, Battery G • 34th New York Battery

FOURTH DIVISION Brig. Gen. Edward Ferrero
First Brigade Col. Joshua K. Sigfried
27th U. S. Colored Troops • 30th U.S. Colored Troops • 39th U.S. Colored Troops
43rd U.S. Colored Troops

Second Brigade Col. Henry G. Thomas
30th Connecticut (colored), detachment • 19th U.S. Colored Troops • 23rd U.S. Colored Troops

Artillery
Pennsylvania, Battery D • 3rd Vermont, Battery

CAVALRY
3rd New Jersey • 22nd New York • 2nd Ohio • 13th Pennsylvania

Reserve Artillery Capt. John Edwards, Jr.
27th New York Battery • 1st Rhode Island Light, Battery D • 1st Rhode Island Light, Battery H
2nd United States, Battery E • 3rd United States, Battery G • 3rd United States, Batteries L and M

Provisional Brigade Col. Elisha G. Marshall
14th New York Heavy Artillery • 24th New York Cavalry (dismounted)
2nd Pennsylvania Provisional Heavy Artillery

ARMY OF NORTHERN VIRGINIA
Gen. Robert E. Lee

FIRST ARMY CORPS Lt. Gen. James Longstreet
KERSHAW'S DIVISION Brig. Gen. Joseph B. Kershaw
Kershaw's Brigade Col. John W. Henagan
2nd South Carolina • 3rd South Carolina • 7th South Carolina • 8th South Carolina • 15th South Carolina • 3rd South Carolina Battalion

Humphreys' Brigade Brig. Gen. Benjamin G. Humphreys
13th Mississippi • 17th Mississippi • 18th Mississippi • 21st Mississippi

Wofford's Brigade Brig. Gen. William T. Wofford
16th Georgia • 18th Georgia • 24th Georgia • Cobb's (Georgia) Legion Phillips (Georgia) Legion • 3rd Georgia Battalion Sharpshooters

Bryan's Brigade Brig. Gen. Goode Bryan
10th Georgia • 50th Georgia • 51st Georgia • 53rd Georgia

FIELD'S DIVISION Maj. Gen. Charles W. Field
Jenkins' Brigade Brig. Gen. Micah Jenkins
1st South Carolina • 2nd South Carolina (Rifles) • 5th South Carolina • 6th South Carolina Palmetto Sharpshooters

Gregg's Brigade Brig. Gen. John Gregg
3rd Arkansas • 1st Texas • 4th Texas • 5th Texas

Law's Brigade Col. William F. Perry
4th Alabama • 15th Alabama • 44th Alabama • 47th Alabama • 48th Alabama

Anderson's Brigade Brig. Gen. George T. Anderson
7th Georgia • 8th Georgia • 9th Georgia • 11th Georgia • 59th Georgia

Benning's Brigade Brig. Gen. Henry L. Benning
2nd Georgia • 15th Georgia • 17th Georgia • 20th Georgia

ARTILLERY Brig. Gen. E. Porter Alexander
Huger's Battalion Lt. Col. Frank Huger
Fickling's (South Carolina) battery • Moody's (Louisiana) battery • Parker's (Virginia) battery Smith's (Virginia) battery • Taylor's (Virginia) battery • Woolfolk's (Virginia) battery

Haskell's Battalion Maj. John C. Haskell
Flanner's (North Carolina) battery • Garden's (South Carolina) battery • Lamkin's (Virginia) battery • Ramsay's (North Carolina) battery

Cabell's Battalion Col. Henry C. Cabell
*Callaway's (Georgia) battery • Carlton's (Georgia) battery • McCarthy's (Virginia) battery
Manly's (North Carolina) battery*

SECOND ARMY CORPS Lt. Gen. Richard S. Ewell
EARLY'S DIVISION Maj. Gen. Jubal A. Early
Pegram's Brigade Brig. Gen. John Pegram
13th Virginia • 31st Virginia • 49th Virginia • 52nd Virginia • 58th Virginia

Johnston's Brigade Brig. Gen. Robert D. Johnston
5th North Carolina • 12th North Carolina • 20th North Carolina • 23rd North Carolina

Gordon's Brigade Brig. Gen. John B. Gordon
13th Georgia • 26th Georgia • 31st Georgia • 38th Georgia • 60th Georgia • 61st Georgia

Hays's Brigade Brig. Gen. Harry T. Hays
5th Louisiana • 6th Louisiana • 7th Louisiana • 8th Louisiana • 9th Louisiana

JOHNSON'S DIVISION Maj. Gen. Edward "Allegheny" Johnson
Stonewall Brigade Brig. Gen. James A. Walker
2nd Virginia • 4th Virginia • 5th Virginia • 27th Virginia • 33rd Virginia

Jones's Brigade Brig. Gen. John M. "Rum" Jones
21st Virginia • 25th Virginia • 42nd Virginia • 44th Virginia • 48th Virginia • 50th Virginia

Steuart's Brigade Brig. Gen. George H. "Maryland" Steuart
1st North Carolina • 3rd North Carolina • 10th Virginia • 23rd Virginia • 37th Virginia

Stafford's Brigade Brig. Gen. Leroy A. Stafford
1st Louisiana • 2nd Louisiana • 10th Louisiana • 14th Louisiana • 15th Louisiana

RODES'S DIVISION MAJ. GEN. ROBERT E. RODES
DANIEL'S BRIGADE Brig. Gen. Junius Daniel
*32nd North Carolina • 43rd North Carolina • 45th North Carolina • 53rd North Carolina
2nd North Carolina Battalion*

Ramseur's Brigade Brig. Gen. Stephen D. Ramseur
2nd North Carolina • 4th North Carolina • 14th North Carolina • 30th North Carolina

Battle's Brigade Brig. Gen. Cullen A. Battle
3rd Alabama • 5th Alabama • 6th Alabama • 12th Alabama • 26th Alabama

Doles's Brigade Brig. Gen. George Doles
4th Georgia • 12th Georgia • 44th Georgia

ARTILLERY Brig. Gen. Armistead L. Long
Braxton's Battalion Lt. Col. Carter M. Braxton
Carpenter's (Virginia) battery • Cooper's (Virginia) battery • Hardwicke's (Virginia) battery

Nelson's Battalion Lt. Col. William Nelson
Kirkpatrick's (Virginia) battery • Massie's (Virginia) battery • Milledge's (Georgia) battery

Page's Battalion Maj. Richard C. M. Page
*W. P. Carter's (Virginia) battery • Fry's (Virginia) battery • Page's (Virginia) battery
Reese's (Alabama) battery*

Cutshaw's Battalion Maj. Wilfred E. Cutshaw
Carrington's (Virginia) battery • A. W. Garber's (Virginia), battery • Tanner's (Virginia) battery

Hardaway's Battalion Lt. Col. Robert A. Hardaway
*Dance's (Virginia) battery • Graham's (Virginia) battery • C. B. Griffin's (Virginia) battery
Jones's (Virginia) battery • B. H. Smith's (Virginia), battery*

THIRD ARMY CORPS Lt. Gen. Ambrose P. Hill
ANDERSON'S DIVISION Maj. Gen. Richard H. Anderson
Perrin's Brigade Brig. Gen. Abner Perrin
8th Alabama • 9th Alabama • 10th Alabama • 11th Alabama • 14th Alabama

Mahone's Brigade Brig. Gen. William Mahone
6th Virginia • 12th Virginia • 16th Virginia • 41st Virginia • 61st Virginia

Harris's Brigade Brig. Gen. Nathaniel H. Harris
12th Mississippi • 16th Mississippi • 19th Mississippi • 48th Mississippi

Perry's Brigade Brig. Gen. Edward A. Perry
2nd Florida • 5th Florida • 8th Florida

Wright's Brigade Brig. Gen. Ambrose R. Wright
3rd Georgia • 22nd Georgia • 48th Georgia • 2nd Georgia Battalion

HETH'S DIVISION Maj. Gen. Henry Heth
Davis's Brigade Col. John M. Stone
2nd Mississippi • 11th Mississippi • 42nd Mississippi • 55th North Carolina

Cooke's Brigade Brig. Gen. John R. Cooke
15th North Carolina • 27th North Carolina • 46th North Carolina • 48th North Carolina

Walker' s Brigade Brig. Gen. Henry H. Walker
40th Virginia • 47th Virginia • 55th Virginia • 22nd Virginia Battalion

Archer's Brigade Brig. Gen. James J. Archer[1]
13th Alabama • 1st Tennessee (Provisional Army) • 7th Tennessee • 14th Tennessee

Kirkland's Brigade Brig. Gen. William W. Kirkland
*11th North Carolina • 26th North Carolina • 44th North Carolina • 47th North Carolina
52nd North Carolina*

WILCOX'S DIVISION Maj. Gen. Cadmus M. Wilcox
Lane's Brigade Brig. Gen. James H. Lane
*7th North Carolina • 18th North Carolina • 28th North Carolina • 33rd North Carolina
37th North Carolina*

McGowan's Brigade Brig. Gen. Samuel McGowan
*1st South Carolina (Provisional) • 12th South Carolina • 13th South Carolina
14th South Carolina • 1st South Carolina (Orr's Rifles)*

Scales's Brigade Brig. Gen. Alfred M. Scales
*13th North Carolina • 16th North Carolina • 22nd North Carolina • 34th North Carolina
38th North Carolina*

Thomas's Brigade Brig. Gen. Edward R. Thomas
14th Georgia • 35th Georgia • 45th Georgia • 49th Georgia

ARTILLERY Col. R. Lindsay Walker
Poague's Battalion Lt. Col. William T. Poague
*Richards's (Mississippi) battery • Utterback's (Virginia) battery
Williams's (North Carolina) battery • Wyatt's (Virginia) battery*

Pegram's Battalion Lt. Col. William J. Pegram
*Brander's (Virginia) battery • Cayce's (Virginia) battery • Ellett's (Virginia) battery
Marye's (Virginia) battery • Zimmerman's (South Carolina) battery*

McIntosh's Battalion Lt. Col. David G. McIntosh
*Clutter's (Virginia) battery • Donald's (Virginia) battery • Hurt's (Alabama) battery
Price's (Virginia) battery*

Richardson's Battalion Lt. Col. Charles Richardson
*Grandy's (Virginia) battery • Landry's (Louisiana) battery • Moore's (Virginia) battery
Penick's (Virginia) battery*

Cutts's Battalion Col. Allen S. Cutts
Patterson's (Georgia) battery • Ross's (Georgia) battery • Wingfield's (Georgia) battery

CAVALRY CORPS Maj. Gen. James E. B. Stuart
HAMPTON'S DIVISION Maj. Gen. Wade Hampton
Young's Brigade Brig. Gen. Pierce M. B. Young
7th Georgia • Cobb's (Georgia) Legion • Phillips (Georgia) Legion • 20th Georgia Battalion
Jeff Davis (Mississippi) Legion

Butler's Brigade Brig. Gen. Matthew C. Butler
4th South Carolina • 5th South Carolina • 6th South Carolina

Rosser's Brigade Brig. Gen. Thomas L. Rosser
7th Virginia • 11th Virginia • 12th Virginia • 35th Virginia Battalion

FITZHUGH LEE'S DIVISION Maj. Gen. Fitzhugh Lee
Lomax's Brigade Brig. Gen. Lunsford L. Lomax
5th Virginia • 6th Virginia • 15th Virginia

Wickham's Brigade Brig. Gen. Williams C. Wickham
1st Virginia • 2nd Virginia • 3rd Virginia • 4th Virginia

WILLIAM H. F. LEE'S DIVISION Maj. Gen. William H. F. Lee
Chambliss' Brigade Brig. Gen. John R. Chambliss
9th Virginia • 10th Virginia • 13th Virginia

Gordon's Brigade Brig. Gen. James B. Gordon
1st North Carolina • 2nd North Carolina • 5th North Carolina

HORSE ARTILLERY Maj. R. Preston Chew
Breathed's Battalion Maj. James Breathed
Hart's (South Carolina) battery • Johnston's (Virginia) battery • McGregor's (Virginia) battery
Shoemaker's (Virginia) battery • Thomson's (Virginia) battery

----

1 During the battle, these troops fought under the command of Brig. Gen. Henry H. Walker alongside the troops of Walker's Brigade.

Artillery in Tapp Field (cm)

Bloody Promenade: Reflections on a Civil War Battle
Stephen Cushman
University of Virginia Press (1999)
ISBN-13: 978-0813920412

At times elegant, at times as impenetrable as the Wilderness itself, poet Stephen Cushman's personal reflections on the Wilderness offer unique lenses through which to view the battle, the ecosystem, the landscape, and the battlefield.

The Wilderness Campaign
Gary Gallagher, ed.
University of North Carolina Press (1997)
ISBN-13: 978-0807823347

Gary Gallagher's essay collections on the Eastern Theater battles always offer a multitude of delectable goodies, but his Wilderness volume is a veritable who's-who of Civil War all-stars, with essays by Brooks Simpson, John Hennessy, Gordon Rhea, Peter Carmichael, Bob Krick, Carol Reardon, and Robert E. L. Krick, plus Gallagher himself.

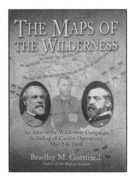

The Maps of the Wilderness: An Atlas of the Wilderness Campaign, May 2-7, 1864
Bradley Gottfried
Savas Beatie (2016)
ISBN-13: 978-1611212587

Leave it to Bradley Gottfried to lay open "the dark, close wood" in a way that makes sense of time, space, and wilderness. His latest entry in the Savas Beatie Military Atlas Series, *Maps of the Wilderness*, carries on his fine tradition of bringing clarity to complexity.

The Battle of the Wilderness in Myth and Memory: Reconsidering Virginia's Most Notorious Civil War Battlefield
Adam Petty
LSU Press (2019)
ISBN-13: 978-0807171912

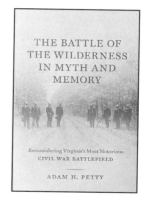

Adam H. Petty's systematic study examines the mythic power of the Wilderness as a thing unto itself, as described by soldiers during three major campaigns: Chancellorsville, Mine Run, and the Overland Campaign. In doing so, Petty casts light into that dark foliage and explains how the Wilderness grew in soldiers' imaginations and why it still has such power over our own.

The Battle of the Wilderness, May 5-6, 1864
Gordon Rhea
LSU (2004)
ISBN-13: 978-0807130216

The first volume in Gordon Rhea's definitive study of the Overland Campaign made a huge splash when it first appeared, and it set the stage for equally incredible volumes that followed. The Battle of the Wilderness remains the go-to study for serious students of the campaign's first engagement.

A Season of Slaughter: The Battle of Spotsylvania Court House, May 8-21, 1864
Chris Mackowski and Kristopher D. White • Savas Beatie (2013) • ISBN-13: 978-1611211481

Strike Them a Blow: Battle Along the North Anna River, May 21-25, 1864
Chris Mackowski • Savas Beatie (2015) • ISBN-13: 978-1611212549

Hurricane from the Heavens: The Battle of Cold Harbor, May 26 - June 5, 1864
Daniel T. Davis and Philip S. Greenwalt • Savas Beatie (2014) • ISBN-13: 978-1611211870

No Turning Back: A Guide to the 1864 Overland Campaign, from the Wilderness to Cold Harbor, May 4 - June 13, 1864
Robert Dunkerly, Donald Pfanz, and David Ruth
Savas Beatie (2014) • ISBN-13: 978-1611211931

What begins in *Hell Itself* continues on in *A Season of Slaughter* at Spotsylvania Court House, then shifts to the banks of the North Anna River for *Strike Them a Blow*, and finally ends with a *Hurricane from the Heavens* at Cold Harbor. Follow the Overland Campaign volume by volume. Or, to drive the entire route of the armies from the Rapidan River to the James, pick up *No Turning Back* as the perfect travel companion.

About the Author

Chris Mackowski, Ph.D., is

· the editor-in-chief of Emerging Civil War (www.emergingcivilwar.com)

· a writing professor in the Jandoli School Communication at St. Bonaventure University

· a former historian with Fredericksburg and Spotsylvania National Military Park, which includes the Wilderness battlefield

· the historian-in-residence at Stevenson Ridge, a historic property located on the Spotsylvania Court House battlefield (www.stevensonridge.com)

· the author or co-author of 17 books on the Civil War

· grateful that you have taken the time to stay connected to America's history and the story of the American Civil War

· hopeful that you will support battlefield preservation